Creating
INCLUSIVE
Learning Environments
for YOUNG
CHILDREN

This book is dedicated
to four very special people:
my husband and best friend, Michael Willis;
my first and best teacher, Jessie Clarice Hightower;
my daughter, Kimberly Michelle Davis; and
my dear niece, Lindsey West, who has
taught me that cerebral palsy is only
a minor inconvenience and not
an insurmountable obstacle.

Creating INCLUSIVE Learning Environments for YOUNG CHILDREN

What to Do on Monday Morning

Clarissa Willis

CORWIN PRESS

A SAGE Company

For information:

Corwin Press
A SAGE Company
2455 Teller Road
Thousand Oaks, California 91320
www.corwinpress.com

SAGE Ltd.
1 Oliver's Yard
55 City Road
London, EC1Y 1SP
United Kingdom

SAGE India Pvt. Ltd.
B 1/I 1 Mohan Cooperative
   Industrial Area
Mathura Road, New Delhi 110 044
India

SAGE Asia-Pacific Pte. Ltd.
33 Pekin Street #02-01
Far East Square
Singapore 048763

Printed in the United States of America.

Library of Congress Cataloging-in-Publication Data

Willis, Clarissa.
  Creating inclusive learning environments for young children : what to
do on Monday morning / Clarissa Willis.
      p. cm.
  Includes bibliographical references and index.
  ISBN 978-1-4129-5718-2 (cloth : acid-free paper) —
  ISBN 978-1-4129-5719-9 (pbk. : acid-free paper)
  1. Children with disabilities—Education. 2. Early childhood special
education. 3. Inclusive education. I. Title.
  LC4015.W55 2009
  371.9'0472—dc22

                         2008004867

This book is printed on acid-free paper.

08 09 10 11 10 9 8 7 6 5 4 3 2 1

Acquisitions Editor:	Stacey Wagner
Managing Editor:	Jessica Allan
Editorial Assistant:	Joanna Coelho
Production Editor:	Appingo Publishing Services
Cover Designer:	Monique Hahn

Contents

Acknowledgments

This book would not have been possible without the help of some very dedicated professionals who have advised, directed, critiqued, and guided my work.

Dr. Rebecca T. Isbell, the Director of the Center of Excellence at East Tennessee State University, an expert in how children learn and how to craft an appropriate environment for all children.

Dr. Sheila P. Smith, my resident editor, sounding board, and overall critique committee. Her editing skills, computer expertise, and critiquing skills are paramount in making this book flow and come together seamlessly.

Ms. Marcia Camp for her consultation, advice, and careful proofreading of this manuscript.

Dr. Pam Schiller, author, consultant, and expert on brain research, a mentor who taught me the value of developing, focusing, practicing, and reflecting in the lives of children and adults.

Ms. Sharon MacDonald, author and consultant, for her time, expertise, and willingness to listen, respond, and enlighten.

Ms. Donna Nelson, the Coordinator of Expanding Horizons—Early Intervention Project, whose knowledge and expert advice is always well received.

Ms. Joellyn Smith-Thompson, Graduate Student in Communication Disorders, and my graduate assistant, who made endless trips to the library to verify research, gather information, and check resources.

Mr. Justin Mitchell, Honor Student and humanitarian, who contributed the original artwork to this project.

Mr. Mike Talley, photographer/videographer, for his skill and expertise in capturing children as they participate in inclusive environments.

Last, but certainly not least, the children, families, and teachers at East Tennessee State University Child Development Center and Little

Buccaneers Student Child Care Center and Ms. Museaus' Developmental Pre-K Class at Asbury Center.

Additionally, Corwin Press gratefully acknowledges the following peer reviewers for their editorial insight and guidance:

Suzanne Beane
Preschool Varying Exceptionalities Teacher
Cypress Elementary School
New Port Richey, FL

Kim Hughes
Therapeutic Preschool Teacher/Therapist/Trainer
Project Enlightenment of Wake County Public School System
Raleigh, NC

Toby Karten
Author and Teacher
Graduate Instructor
Gratz College, College of New Jersey
Manalapan, NJ

Mary Kreger
Director of Special Education
District 196
Rosemount, MN

Jane C. Perlmutter
Professor
Western Carolina University
Cullowhee, NC

Lynn Williams, M.Ed.
First Grade Lafayette Elementary
Boulder Valley School District
Lafayette, CO

About the Author

 **Clarissa A. Willis,** PhD, is the author of *Teaching Young Children with Autism Spectrum Disorder* and coauthor of *Inclusive Literacy Lessons for Early Childhood.* In addition she has written adaptations for children with special needs for Wright Group. Dr. Willis has over 30 years' experience working with children with special needs as a speech pathologist, early interventionist, teacher, and grant administrator. As a consultant she has provided workshops and keynote addresses for schools and organizations across the country and abroad. Formerly she was the Associate Director of the Center of Excellence and an Associate Professor of Special Education in the Department of Human Development and Learning at East Tennessee State University. Currently she lives in North Carolina and spends her time writing, speaking, and consulting.

Introduction

Another school year is approaching. Eagerly, you anticipate a new class with students ready to learn all about the wonderful things you have planned. You prepare the classroom, label each cubby or locker, plan the first week of the new school year, and unpack the learning centers you have worked so hard to develop. Now, all you have to do is sit back and wait for that "magical" first day when your new class arrives.

Everything goes according to plan, until . . . Without notice, you are summoned to meet with your center director who informs you that you have been "chosen" to have three children in your class who are atypical. "Okay," you say to yourself, "I can handle this—I'm a well-trained professional, right?" After all, you believe that all children are "special." What you discover, however, is that these "special" children have disabilities such as Asperger syndrome, Down syndrome, or Fragile "X" syndrome. This causes you to pause, since, while you want to welcome everyone into your classroom, you are concerned that these three children might take almost all of your time and energy. You have been told you will receive special inservice training, later in November—but you need to know what to do *now*!

While inclusion of children with special needs with their typically developing peers was once considered a trend, today, it is considered the norm. Many early childhood teachers with years of classroom experience are challenged by the demands of serving children with special needs. The benefits of inclusion, or "blended practices," have been documented in the current research. This book is designed to reach regular early childhood educators who suddenly find themselves teaching children at risk for school failure and children with developmental delays. In addition, this book will serve as a resource for special education teachers who want to learn about additional strategies to use as they help children with special needs function in a regular early childhood setting. Each chapter includes simple strategies, adaptations, and activities that are designed to help teachers address the special needs of the children in their classroom. This book is designed to help you bridge the gap between theory and practice by answering the question that teachers ask most often, "What do I do Monday morning?"

Part I

Children With Special Needs in the Inclusive Classroom

Working With Children With Special Needs

Figure 1.1   Children with special needs learn best in a natural environment.

WHAT DO I NEED TO KNOW TO WORK WITH CHILDREN WITH SPECIAL NEEDS?

As with children in a general education setting, those with special needs have their own unique strengths and weaknesses. Some children may have recognizable disabilities, such as a child with cerebral palsy who is in a wheelchair or a child with vision difficulties who wears glasses. Other children, while not having been diagnosed with a specific disability, may exhibit challenging behaviors that interrupt the daily routine.

Children may have a nonspecific diagnosis, such as *developmental delay.* Pediatricians and other medical professionals often prefer this diagnosis for young children, since it implies that, given time and opportunity, the child may "catch up" in the areas in which they are currently delayed. In other cases, a child may be "at risk" for a disability because of environmental conditions or due to a chronic health condition, such as a depressed immune system or chronic asthma. At risk does not mean that the child has a particular disability; it simply means that there is a high probability that, without intervention, the child will develop a permanent delay.

Regardless of the type of delay a child experiences, it is important to keep in mind that all children can learn and should be allowed to participate in everyday routines and activities to the best of their capabilities. Research tells us that children learn best in natural environments with typically developing peers (Allen & Cowdery, 2005; Brown, Hemmeter, & Pretti-Frontczak, 2005). This interaction not only benefits the child with special needs, but also helps children without special needs learn about tolerance and acceptance of others.

SETTING THE STAGE FOR INCLUSION

Prior to the 1960s, only a few programs served young children with special needs. Most of these "special schools" were residential state schools or were focused on specific disabilities, such as programs for the deaf or blind. Public school programs, if they existed at all, were self-contained programs located in buildings separate from where children without special needs attended school.

One of the most significant breakthroughs for children with special needs occurred in 1965, when Head Start, a program explicitly designed for low-income children and families, was signed into law. The Equal Opportunity Act of 1964 (PL 88-452) was instrumental in a Head Start initiative that was adopted in the early 1970s. This initiative mandated that 10 percent of the Head Start slots would be designated specifically for children with special needs. This was the first time that a federal program had provided incentives for children with special needs to be included in educational environments with their peers. In 1968, another critical piece of legislation was passed, the Handicapped Children's Early Education Program (HCEEP), funded by the U.S. Department of Education. This legislation provided money for states to develop model programs or to replicate existing programs for young children with special needs. These model programs served as the basis for most of the early research on the efficacy or effectiveness of services for young children with special needs.

Public Law 94-142, also called the Education of All Handicapped Children Act of 1975, mandated services for school-age children with disabilities. Under the provisions of this act, services for preschool children were not required but were strongly encouraged through monetary incentives. This act introduced many new terms, including *mainstreaming*, which was used to describe the amount of time each day that a child with special needs participated in a program with peers who did not have special needs. For many children, the time allocated to spend with peers was during recess, lunch, or nonacademic subjects such as music or art. While mainstreaming was a far better alternative than a segregated or self-contained setting, it was still not very inclusive. Some educators seemed to believe that mainstreaming was like inviting someone to visit you for a few minutes or a few hours and then sending them back to their own house. In effect, mainstreaming for many children meant they could visit a regular classroom for a specified amount of time, but they really did not participate in many of the activities that were going on. In fact, some children merely observed, while others learned and interacted with each other. At best, interaction between children with special needs and their typically developing peers was minimal and artificial.

Public Law 94-142, however, did set the stage for subsequent laws that were designed to ensure that all children with special needs received the services to which they were legally entitled. One of the laws was Public Law 99-457, or the Education of the Handicapped Act Amendments, which amended Public Law 94-142 to mandate services for children ages three to five who have a diagnosed special need. Several other amendments have subsequently been put into place and have further strengthened the law and mandate for services for all children. Public Law 101-476, the Individuals with Disabilities Education Act (IDEA), which was later renamed the Individuals with Disabilities Education Improvement Act of 2004 (PL 108-446), outlines very specific guidelines that local school districts are required to adhere to by law when providing for the needs of children with disabilities. The provisions of the act for children age three to twenty-one are the following:

1. Each school district must provide a free and appropriate public education (FAPE). This includes the provision that the child is entitled to all services that are appropriate to meet his educational needs. Examples of related services include, but are not limited to, speech therapy, occupational therapy, and transportation. In addition, these services must be provided without cost to parents. Not all children with disabilities will qualify for all offered services, but each child is entitled to those services that accommodate his particular needs. It should be noted that many school districts do not have programs for three-year-olds. If this is the case, such districts may choose to make a contract with outside child care providers, or with centers where children without special needs may be enrolled.

2. Assessments must be nonbiased and nondiscriminatory. They must be conducted in the child's native language, and most important, educational decisions about a child cannot be made based on a single test. In other words, a variety of assessments is used to determine eligibility for educational services.

3. Once a child has been determined as eligible for services, an educational plan is developed and written by a team that includes the child's family, a special education teacher, and a general education teacher. This team reviews and updates the individual education program (IEP) on an annual basis. The child's IEP clearly outlines what types of service she will receive and how often she will receive the service.

4. The child must receive the service to which he is entitled in an environment that is the least restrictive. Presumed and made clear in the most recent reauthorization of IDEA is that the least restrictive environment (LRE) should be the general education classroom, unless there is justification as to why it would not be appropriate. Again, many school districts elect to make a contract with a private preschool to provide these services. However, because contracting with organizations outside the school is often cost prohibitive, more districts are opting to provide the services themselves.

5. Children from birth to age three with special needs usually receive services through a state-provided comprehensive early intervention system. The child is assigned a service coordinator who works with the family to assess the child, plan appropriate services, and develop an individual family service plan (IFSP). The IFSP is a written plan for services the child will receive, which helps guide the family as the child transitions into other programs. For children, birth to age three, services are provided in the child's *natural environment,* defined as the place where the child might spend time if she did not have a disability. In most cases, the natural environment is at home. However, if both parents work, the natural environment may be a preschool or a private home care provider.

INCLUSION, BLENDING, AND REVERSE MAINSTREAMING

Over time, as children with special needs were observed spending time with their typically developing peers, educators began to recognize that inclusion went beyond mainstreaming. More important, they realized that to fully include a child meant that the child had to become more than an occasional visitor in the classroom. It meant that the child needed to become a member of the classroom community. One method for providing children with special needs with opportunities to be with their peers without special needs was called *reverse mainstreaming.* Children without special needs are placed in a program or educational setting that consists of children with special needs. Reverse mainstreaming is certainly considered a better alternative than segregated programs, but it is still not a fully inclusive program since most of the children in the classroom have special needs.

Because regular early childhood educators and early childhood special education teachers work together in the inclusive program to "blend" aspects of both regular and special education into their programs, the term *blended practices* is often used. However, before practices can be successfully blended, all those working with the child must fully understand the concepts and philosophy behind inclusion.

WHY IS INCLUSION IMPORTANT?

For the past 25 years, a significant body of literature has attested to the positive outcomes for children with special needs who have been placed in settings with their typically developing peers (Brown et al., 2005). Children with special needs who receive related services (special education, speech/language therapy, occupational therapy, etc.) benefit more when those services are provided in the natural environment with their peers (Allen & Cowdery, 2005). Natural environments are settings where children without special needs learn and play. These may include public and private preschool programs. Ongoing research has shown that embedding instruction and therapeutic services within the framework of natural environments is both beneficial to the child and cost effective for the setting (Bailey & McWilliam, 1990; Bricker & Cripe, 1992; Noonan & McCormick, 2000). However, just placing a child with special needs in a setting with his peers does not ensure that "meaningful" inclusion will take place.

WHAT IS "MEANINGFUL" INCLUSION?

The Division of Early Childhood (DEC), a subdivision of the Council for Exceptional Children, is a professional organization dedicated to the field of early childhood special education. The DEC position paper on inclusion states that inclusion is "a value that supports the rights of all children, regardless of their diverse abilities, to participate actively in natural settings within their communities." However, *meaningful* inclusion is much more than just inviting a child with special needs to join a general education class with her peers. Inclusion is a philosophy that embraces a core belief that children with disabilities learn best in typical settings with peers and that the benefits of such programs have far-reaching, long-term effects on *all* the children in such a classroom. In addition, research has shown that children without special needs experience benefits in these blended settings as well (Bricker, 2000; Schwartz, Sandall, Odom, Horn, & Beckman, 2002).

Successful inclusion requires a team approach and commitment from all team members (the regular education teacher, the special education teacher, administrators, assistants, and most important, the child and her family). It is also important that teachers have all the resources necessary to make inclusion a successful endeavor. Resources may include such things as

- time to meet with the special education teacher and review the child's goals for the year;
- additional staff or assistants;
- access to support services, such as speech therapy, occupational therapy, and physical therapy;
- time to plan and implement the necessary curriculum and environmental adaptations that a child might require;
- funding to purchase special equipment that the child will use in the classroom; and
- a clearly defined plan for working with the child's family to enable the child to reach her potential.

HOW DO I DEVELOP A PHILOSOPHY OF MEANINGFUL INCLUSION?

To develop a philosophy and an attitude of full inclusion of all children, several important basics should be understood:

1. Children with disabilities do not need to be "repaired" or "fixed" before they can be included with their peers. This means that you recognize that every child is unique and has worth, regardless of his challenges.
2. Children will be growing up in a society where not everyone is the same. Preschool and kindergarten children are at a developmental stage where they can learn to be tolerant and accepting of others.

3. A successful inclusion program must involve a team approach to the child's education, which means input and ongoing collaborative efforts from all participants (especially the child's family) are welcomed and encouraged.

4. Inclusive programs encompass the belief that all children are entitled to developmentally appropriate materials and exemplary classroom practices that honor the child's strengths as well as weaknesses.

5. One should believe that "one size" does not fit all and no one method, process, or product will work for all children. This includes an understanding that working with children with disabilities is not about using a specific product, but about following a process.

6. Quality programs for children should allow the teacher flexibility to perceive when something works, and for change and adaptation when something does not work. It is all right to recognize when an approach or a method is not working and change it.

GENERAL STRATEGIES FOR WORKING WITH CHILDREN WITH SPECIAL NEEDS

1. Demonstrate that you value each child in your classroom.
    - Children in your classroom hear what you say, watch what you do, and notice how you act. It is important that the other children in your class see that you view all children, especially children with special needs, as valuable class members who are important not only to you but also to each other.
    - Use people-first language when talking about a child. Refer to the child first and the disability last. For example, Davis is a child with Down syndrome; he is not the "Down syndrome child" in your class. Sheila is a child with a visual challenge; she is not a "blind child."
    - When other children ask about a child's disability, answer it honestly and openly. Provide enough information to help the child without special needs see that her classmate learns differently or needs help doing some things. Always explain that everyone can do certain things well and everyone needs help at times.

- Never talk about the child with disabilities as if he is not present. Parents of children with disabilities do not want pity; they want support from people who value what their child can contribute.

2. Help children in general education classes accept their peers with special needs.
   - Recognize the value of partial participation. Plan activities that include all children. Look for ways to help the child with challenges participate in everyday activities and routines. If the child cannot fully participate and do everything exactly like her peers, look for ways to adapt an activity so the child can partially participate.
   - In your classroom, read stories that feature people with disabilities as members of a community and put up pictures that depict people with special needs as active participants within the community. A list of books featuring people with special needs can be found in the appendix.
   - Remind all the children in your classroom that everyone has both strengths and weaknesses. Remember that all children can learn; some just take more time and practice.
   - Clearly demonstrate that you have a "zero tolerance" policy against bullying, teasing, and laughing at others for any reason. Teach children what to do if someone teases them.
   - Do not set up a child for failure; give the child a task he can do before introducing something he is just learning to do. This builds self-esteem and encourages children to try new things.

3. Look for opportunities to help a child learn school survival skills.
   - Preschool is the time when children learn fundamental skills they will use to get along with others. These are often referred to as social skills. Parents often report that one thing lacking in their child's life is friends (Willis, 2006). Learning the skills needed to make friends is especially difficult for children with special needs.
   - Often, a child's inability to communicate her wants and needs makes it difficult for other children to know how to interact with her.
   - Learning how to make friends and keep friends, to interact with others around them, and to ask an adult for assistance are very important "survival" skills in an early childhood setting.

- While most children learn social skills through observation, experience, and play, children with special needs often struggle with social cues. For example, they may not know how to ask another child for a toy or how to join into a playgroup activity. For this reason, they are frequently unable to establish lasting friendships.

4. Aim for the child to become competent in all social situations.

Figure 1.2   Positive social interaction is often difficult for children with special needs.

  - One of the primary goals of most early childhood classrooms is for children to learn to be socially competent. A socially competent child has learned through observation and play what it takes to get along with peers and how to control his own behavior so that others will want to be his friends.
  - Self-confidence is a characteristic of a socially competent child. Because of self-confidence, she is more likely to participate in novel situations, to experiment, and to enjoy new activities.
  - Children learn by observing others. This is often difficult for a child with special needs. He is less likely to imitate the behavior observed in other children, which might ultimately allow him to be more socially accepted by others.

HOW DO I GET THE CHILD'S FAMILY INVOLVED?

Knowing what to say and how to interact with families of children with special needs takes time and practice. Remember that all families want their children to succeed and be happy. Families of children with disabilities have the same concerns as those with children who do not have special needs, on top of the added challenges that other families may not experience. In addition, working with any family involves building a relationship. Be honest when you talk about the child, and remember that families want to hear about what the child can do as well as her challenges. It is also important to note that families may be from diverse cultures or backgrounds and that the definition of family has expanded to be, in itself, more inclusive and diverse. Guidelines for working with family members are as follows:

- Work under the assumption that parents are almost always doing the best they can at the moment. Sometimes parents may make choices that we feel are not in the best interest of the child; unless you have a child with disabilities, you can never truly understand the perspective of parents who do. As the child's teacher, you can empathize and try to appreciate how parents might feel, but you can never really know the day-to-day realities of living with and caring for a child with special needs. Therefore, unless your own child has special needs, avoid saying things like, "I know just how you feel" or "If it were my child, I would feel just as you do."
- Parents view their child as a valued member of the family unit. To a family member, a child with special needs is not just a child with disabilities; he is much more. Parents of these children have the same aspirations for their children as other parents do.
- Respect the opinion of a parent, even if you do not agree with it. Parents often suggest that the main thing a teacher can do to understand their perspective is to treat them as equal partners in the decision-making process.
- Establish rapport by being a resource they can count on. Teachers can help parents by making sure they are aware of the resources available to them.

RESOURCES FOR FAMILIES

1. Access to support services, such as physical therapy, speech/language therapy, or special education services
2. Information about local support groups for families of children with disabilities; such groups can help parents realize they are not alone, and can provide tremendous support

3. Suggestions about where parents might go to obtain adaptive equipment or specialized materials for their child, such as eyeglasses or hearing aids

4. Contact information for potential government resources, which may entitle them to certain benefits

5. Information about where to locate respite care (a place where the child can go for a day or a few days, so the parents can have a break)

WORKING TO "ENABLE" AND "EMPOWER" FAMILIES

The value of enabling and empowering families to become self-advocates is well documented in special education literature. When you *enable* a family, you give them the tools they need to make informed decisions; when you *empower* them, you show them how to use those tools. What this means is that you provide an avenue through which parents learn to access the resources and tools available to them to advocate for their child. Demonstrate that you are a team member who values their child by

- using words that show you are a team member—for example, words like we and us instead of me and you;
- being positive and referring to their child's special needs as challenges, not as weaknesses;
- listening carefully, and asking family members what they think—then, respecting what they say; and
- showing family members that you consider their child a valuable community member by using the child's name when you talk about her.

TERMS USED IN THIS CHAPTER

adaptive equipment—specialized equipment that enables a person with special needs to complete a task that he would be unable to complete without such equipment.

blended practices—the combining of practices that can be used to address the needs of all children in inclusive settings. This term usually means that regular early childhood practices and early childhood special education practices are blended in such a way that all children learn and participate in classroom activities.

developmental delays—used by physicians to describe a condition in which a child is behind in reaching developmental milestones. Often, this term is used when the physician is unsure whether the child just needs extra help to "catch up" or whether the child may develop more pronounced characteristics of a specific disability.

free and appropriate public education (FAPE)—mandated by law, this refers to the entitlement of every child, who has a diagnosed disability, to a free public education that is appropriate for her needs.

inclusion—used to describe a setting where all children are valued members of the classroom community.

individual education program (IEP)—a plan, written with input from the child's teachers and parents, that outlines the educational goals for the child during a given period (usually one academic year). The IEP must also include how the goals will be met and what services will be provided to the child to help meet these goals.

individual family service plan (IFSP)—The IFSP differs from the IEP in that it is written for a child from birth to age 3 and outlines goals and objectives for the child's overall development. The IFSP is strongly linked to the priorities of the child's family and their needs as well.

least restrictive environment (LRE)—mandated by law, the LRE is the environment that is least restrictive for the child to learn and develop. In most cases, the LRE is a setting where the child spends much of his time with peers without special needs. A statement of the LRE for the child is a mandatory component in the individual education program (IEP).

mainstreaming—when a child with special needs spends part of the day with peers in a general education setting and then returns to a self-contained setting for the remainder of the day.

natural environment—the environment most like the environment where children work, learn, and play.

partial participation—the philosophy that a child participates in an activity as much as possible, even if he cannot finish or complete the activity.

people-first language—describing people with special needs as people, first. For example, one might refer to a child as "Melissa, a child with a hearing impairment," rather than "Melissa, the deaf child."

respite care—care, usually overnight care, which is provided for a person with special needs so that the normal caretaker can be relieved on his duties for a period of time.

reverse mainstreaming—when children without special needs are placed in a program where the majority of the children have special needs.

social skills—skills needed to be social and make friends. Social skills might include such things as greeting a friend, asking to play with others, waiting for a turn, asking for something without hitting or biting, and so forth.

socially competent—a child who is very skilled in interacting socially with others.

RESOURCES USED IN THIS CHAPTER

Allen, K. E., & Cowdery, G. F. (2004). *The exceptional child: Inclusion in early childhood.* Albany, NY: Delmar.

Bailey, D., & McWilliam, R. (1990). *Factors influencing child engagement in mainstream settings.* Washington, DC: Special Education Programs.

Bricker, D., & Woods Cripe, J. J. (1992). *Activity-based approach to early intervention.* Baltimore: Paul H. Brookes.

Bricker, D. (2000). Inclusion: How the scene has changed. *Topics in Early Childhood Special Education, 20*(1), 14–19.

Brown, J. G., Hemmeter, M. L., & Pretti-Frontczak, K. (2005). *Blended practices for teaching young children in inclusive settings.* Baltimore: Paul H. Brookes.

Division of Early Childhood. (1996). *Position paper on inclusion.* Missoula, MT: Author.

Filler, J., & Xu, Y. (2006). Including children with disabilities in early childhood education programs: Individualizing developmentally appropriate practices. *Childhood Education, 83*(2), 92–99.

Noonan, M. J., & McCormick, L. (2000). Practices of co-teaching in inclusive preschool classroom. *NHSA Dialog, 3,* 258–273.

Schwartz, I. S., Sandall, S. R., Odom. S. L., Horn, E., & Beckman, P. J. (2002). I know it when I see it: In search of a common definition of inclusions. In S. L. Odom (Ed.), *Widening the circle: Including children with disabilities in preschool programs* (pp. 10–24). New York: Teachers College Press.

Willis, C. (2006). *Teaching young children with autism spectrum disorder.* Beltsville, MD: Gryphon House.

SUGGESTED READING

Macy, M., & Bricker, D. (2007). Embedding individualized social goals into routine activities in inclusive early childhood classrooms. *Early Child Development and Care, 177*(2), 107–120.

McCormick, L., Noonan, M. J., Ogata, V., & Heck, R. (2001). Co-teacher relationship and program quality implications for preparing teachers for inclusive preschool settings. *Education and Training in Mental Retardation and Developmental Disabilities, 36*(2), 119–132.

Odom, S., Zercher, C., Li, S., Marquart, J., Sandall, S., & Brown, W. (2006). Social acceptance and rejection of preschool children with disabilities: A mixed-method analysis. *Journal of Education Psychology, 98*(4), 807–823.

THE RESEARCH SAYS . . .

Developmentally Appropriate Practices Must Apply to Everyone

The authors looked at inclusion in the context of developmentally appropriate practices. Developmentally appropriate practice (DAP) as defined by National Association of Education for Young Children (NAEYC) is considered the foundation of early childhood education and serves as a guideline for planning a quality curriculum. The NAEYC defined DAP in three dimensions: (1) child development and learning; (2) understanding the individual child and the variables in learning and abilities; and (3) a knowledge of the child's social and cultural environment (Bredekamp & Copple, 1997, p. 9). The authors looked at DAP as it relates to children from different cultures as well as children with diverse abilities. They feel that both the curricula and the instructional models used must reflect these differences.

The authors cite the work of Noonan and McCormick (1993), who noted the importance of understanding the child's social environment. They concluded, "children with a range of disabilities, including those with severe cognitive, motor, emotional, and behavioral disabilities, are a valuable aspect of the differences that we celebrate in our early childhood education programs." In addition the authors discuss the value in taking a closer look at what we believe about how all children grow and learn and how we teach them. This article clearly demonstrates the value of full participation in inclusive settings where educators, administrators, related service professionals, and parents adhere to the philosophy that achievement requires that we emphasize the uniqueness of each child.

Filler, J., & Xu, Y. (2006). Including children with disabilities in early childhood education programs: individualizing developmentally appropriate practices. *Childhood Education, 83*(2), 92–99.

Blending the World of Special Education With General Education Services

2

Figure 2.1   Provide opportunities for children to work together.

BEST PRACTICES ACCORDING TO NAEYC AND DEC

Two professional organizations, the National Association for the Education of Young Children (NAEYC) and the Division of Early Childhood (DEC), have had a major influence on early childhood education and practices for children with and without special needs. The Division of Early Childhood (DEC), as previously mentioned in Chapter 1, is devoted to best practices and research related to young children with special needs. NAEYC is the largest professional organization in the world; its membership is comprised of people who work with young children in many different capacities. Both organizations have best practice guidelines that were developed through years of research and input from practitioners in the field.

According to the NAEYC (2006) Universal Standards, the term *all children* means that every child, regardless of his special needs, should be given the same consideration. Similarly, the *NAEYC Policy Statement on Best Practices* emphasizes that the trend toward including children with special needs in general education settings with their peers must be reflected in all best practice recommendations. Both organizations recommend that quality programs for all children must utilize developmentally appropriate practices, with an emphasis on the following:

- Child development principles;
- Assessment that is authentic and appropriate;
- Considering the child in the context of his family; and
- The importance and value of adequate personnel preparation for people entering the field, as well as ongoing professional development for those already working with children.

In addition, DEC has best practice recommendations in technology as well as in interdisciplinary models of service delivery. Technology, as it relates to children with special needs, is often referred to as assistive technology, which is defined as any item that supports or helps children with special needs gain greater independence. For example, assistive technology may include items that enable a child to perform tasks that she was not able to do previously, such as painting with an adaptive paintbrush or putting together a puzzle with an adaptive knob or handle. In some cases, the technology is more sophisticated and may include devices, such as an adaptive switch or keyboard, that allow the child to use the computer or turn on a battery-operated toy.

Interdisciplinary models of service delivery consist of professionals from different disciplines who plan educational programming for the child. For example, Lucas is a three-year-old child with Down syndrome. For him to function as independently as possible, the annual goals and objectives for his individual education program (IEP) might come from several disciplines; his communication goals would include suggestions from the speech pathologist; his motor skill goals might be developed with input from his physical therapist; and his social skill goals would be established using input from his special education teacher, his regular education teacher, and his family. Working together, this team plans goals to address his overall needs, shares his progress with each other, and meets on a regular basis to talk about any new challenges that he might encounter.

Notice that, in the previous discussion, the family is included in the IEP planning; it is important to understand that no interdisciplinary team is complete without input from the child's family. The perspective of family members is invaluable to learn the child's habits and motivations, be aware of such things as times during the day when the child is most active and alert, offer suggestions as to how to motivate him to try new activities, and learn which skills they believe are most important for him to learn first. Also, the child will be much more

Figure 2.2   Assistive technology helps children with special needs communicate.

successful in learning new skills if he has opportunities to practice his new skills both at school and at home. Research has shown a direct relationship between how well a child learns a new task and the importance of that task to his family members (Driessen, Smit, & Sleegers, 2005).

Combining guidelines from the NAEYC and DEC is an effective way to truly blend a program so that all children have the potential to learn and grow. It is important to note that some practitioners feel that the fields of early childhood and special education have two opposing philosophies. Early childhood teachers are taught to use a constructivist approach, wherein children construct knowledge from their experiences and activities. In contrast, special education teachers may be instructed to use techniques that are more direct, using specific behavior modification tactics to guide instruction for children with special needs. Despite how someone is trained, these two philosophies can be blended effectively in an inclusive classroom.

CONSTRUCTIVISM VERSUS BEHAVIORISM: BLENDING WITHOUT IGNORING BEST PRACTICE

Most early childhood educators follow the constructivist belief that children need challenging opportunities to explore new activities and environments that allow them to develop "constructs" or beliefs about how things work. While Piaget and Vygotsky are considered the fathers of constructivist thinking, much of the later work has been done by Bruner. His work has led to the theory that learning is a process in which children construct or build new ideas or concepts based upon their current or past knowledge. However, advocates of constructivism believe that it is not the environment or an individual activity that facilitates the development of these constructs, but how well the child can mentally process the information that the brain receives (Harnard, 1982). For this reason, some children with special needs are unable to learn the mental processes needed to build on current or past knowledge. In addition, many of these children cannot generalize well. In other words, they have difficulty transferring information from one setting to another or from one person to another. For example, Darren, a typically developing four-year-old, plays with blocks in the manipulative center of his preschool classroom. When Darren visits a friend who has similar blocks, Darren will apply his past knowledge about blocks to the situation. Darren and his friend can play with the blocks in the same way that Darren played with them in his classroom. Thus, Darren can generalize that the blocks at his friend's house are similar to the blocks at school; therefore, they will work in the same manner. This generalization across objects and settings is a mental process that is very difficult for children with special needs, especially those who are cognitively challenged. Bruner (Kearsley, 1999) provides the following summary of the principles of constructivist learning:

1. Readiness—The child must have the skills needed to complete a task and instruction must be concerned with the experiences and contexts that the child needs to be able to learn.
2. If the task or activity is too difficult or if the child does not have the past experiences to help her process what she needs to do to complete the task, it can essentially set the child up to fail and discourage future exploration of new activities.

3. Past knowledge and problem-solving skills help the child solve new problems that are more complex.

Advocates of constructivism also believe that teachers must think about the knowledge and experiences that their students have already developed before planning to introduce a new activity. In other words, children use what they already know to help them connect the new activity to a previously learned activity. Often, children with special needs lack the skills to make these kinds of connections. For that reason, some of the tenets of behaviorism can combine with the views of constructivists so that children with special needs achieve their full learning potential.

Behaviorists, on the other hand, believe that teachers must first know what knowledge or skills children should acquire and then develop a curriculum that is designed to help the child acquire those skills. In other words, they believe that learning results in a permanent change in behavior, which is brought about through experience (Huitt & Hummel, 2006). While early childhood teachers are taught to use constructivist principles and special educators are generally taught to view the child in behaviorist terms, it does not mean that there will be opposing philosophies in an inclusive classroom. In reality, a combination of both approaches can be effective. In fact, three constructs of behaviorism fit nicely into a constructivist classroom: successive approximation, modeling, and cueing. These techniques make activities more meaningful for children with special needs:

1. Successive approximation or shaping is a technique used to encourage a child to attempt a new task. He is reinforced for each attempt. This praise, or reward, helps him keep trying to achieve a new goal.

2. Modeling is often used in the early childhood classroom to show the learner how to do a task. There is always the expectation that the learner can copy the model. When modeling a new task or activity for a child with special needs, it is very helpful if the teacher breaks down the task into smaller steps and invites the child to repeat each step after it is demonstrated.

3. Cueing is a technique that gives the child clues about what she is expected to do. It is used when the teacher provides a clue or cues the child to help remind her what she is supposed to do. For example, if Kara always runs into a learning center instead of waiting her turn, the teacher might place a hand on Kara's shoulder to cue her to wait until it is her turn.

USING OBSERVATION SKILLS TO GUIDE INSTRUCTION

Direct observation is one of the best methods you can use to help in plan-ning activities for children with special needs. The following guidelines will help you know what to observe and how to document it:

1. Select a method for recording your observation that is easy and convenient to use. For example, use color-coded index cards that have a hole punched in the right-hand corner and are held together by a single adjustable ring. Using these cards allows you to write down your observations and notes about a child. Date the cards and attach them to your belt loop or hang them on a pegboard. Whatever method you use, always put the date and time on each observational note.

2. Practice observing what the child is saying, doing, and how he is acting. Record exactly what you hear and see, not what you feel. Avoid making broad generalizations, such as "Ryan always kicks other children." Instead, record, "Ryan kicked Jasper when Jasper tried to play with a truck that Ryan was playing with."

3. Write down your observations as close as possible to the time they occur. Waiting until the end of the school day may result in forgetting important details or information.

4. Describe the context of the child's behavior and actions. For example, you might make a notation such as "Emily left small group today and crawled under the table instead of going to center time."

5. While observing the child, you may see something that you want to further examine. For example, if you notice that the child always seems to play more cooperatively before lunch than after, you may want to make a note to yourself to observe him for a few days before lunch to see if this behavior indicates a pattern.

6. Try to observe the child in a variety of settings and at different times during the day, as this will give you multiple opportunities to document not only what happens but also when it happens.

PLANNING FOR AN IEP MEETING

Federal law mandates that all children with a documented special need have an IEP. This plan is established in consultation with the child's family as well as others who might work with the child such as the special educa-tion teacher and/or a speech pathologist. The IEP reflects the educational and behavior goals for that child during the school year. It is also mandated

THE TEACHER'S RULES OF THE ROAD

- Everyone is a member of the class. Each member of the class has the same rights and responsibilities as his classmates; the expectations for him are matched to his abilities.

- Treat others the way you want them to treat you. Model how to be a friend and how friends act toward each other.

- Consistency and structure work best for children with special needs. While flexibility is very important, it is also important to remember that children with special needs can become very upset and frustrated when people are inconsistent with them and when schedules are disrupted.

- Everyone can participate in some way. Even students with severe disabilities can partially participate in activities.

- All children have strengths and weaknesses. Learn to identify a child's strengths and plan activities that are geared to enhance her strengths.

- Nothing is free and no one is automatically entitled to anything. Communication is perhaps the most important social skill of all. Teach children how to ask for what they want and need verbally, by using signs, or with gestures.

- Learned helplessness cannot be tolerated. In other words, just because a child has a disability or is challenged in some way does not mean that he cannot learn to be as independent as possible. When everything is done for a child he will learn how to be helpless and automatically expect the adults in his world to do things for him.

- Children learn from each other. Arrange the environment so that children have many opportunities to practice new skills, work in groups, and depend on each other to help solve problems.

- Aggression, bullying, and making fun of others are never acceptable. What may seem like simple childish teasing can soon become bullying, which can be frightening for a child with special needs.

- Many times, misbehaviors are just misdirected attempts to communicate. When a child throws an object or has a tantrum, look at the reason behind the action. While the behavior is not acceptable, the reason for the behavior may be explainable and is oftentimes avoidable.

that each child's IEP be reviewed at least once a year and that new goals be written for each year. As the child's teacher, you will be expected to participate in these meetings. Here are a few suggestions regarding how to prepare for an IEP meeting:

- Review the child's assessment data, noting when her last formal assessment was given and what the results were.
- Bring any anecdotal records or notes that you have about how the child is progressing.
- Be prepared to discuss with the planning team those things that you believe are the child's strengths, as well as any challenges you are facing.
- If you keep a portfolio for the child, bring it along, too. This way, you can document her progress in your class.
- Remember to use people-first language when you talk about the child, and don't forget to refer to the child by name whenever possible.

RELATED SERVICES

Under the Individuals with Disabilities Education Act (IDEA), students who qualify for special education services may also be entitled to related services. Related services include transportation and any developmental, corrective, and supported services that are necessary to allow the student to benefit from special education. A school district is not required to provide services necessary to maximize a child's potential. Schools, however, are required to ensure that a student can benefit from special education. They can provide services directly or contract with other agencies to provide related services.

The federal regulations include a long list of related services that schools may provide to students who need them. It is important to note, however, that this list is not exhaustive and may not include all the services that a school district may be required to provide. If the student requires a service that is not on the list, such as an interpreter, the service must still be provided by the school, as long as the service is necessary for the student to be able to benefit from special education. Related services might include some or all of the following:

- Audiology—an audiologist is a specialist who identifies hearing loss and subsequently may provide activities, such as language therapy, auditory training, speech reading, hearing evaluation, and the fitting and adjustment of a hearing aid.

- Counseling services—these services are provided by qualified social workers, psychologists, or guidance counselors and may help the child with one-on-one sessions or group therapy, when warranted.
- Medical services—medical diagnostic services provided by a licensed physician may become the school's responsibility if the child has a medically related disability that results in a need for special education and related services.
- Occupational therapy—occupational therapists are responsible for helping the child improve or restore motor functions that have been impaired or lost. In addition, they help the child learn to do everyday tasks that are necessary for independence.
- Orientation and mobility services—some children with vision loss require the services of personnel who are specially trained to enable those students to become oriented to and move safely within their environment.
- Physical therapy—a physical therapist uses specially designed exercises and equipment to help children regain or improve their physical movements.
- Psychological services—the role of the school psychologist is to administer psychological tests and consult with other school personnel who are involved in meeting the special needs of children. Psychologists also help plan and implement behavior programs for children with emotional or social issues.
- Speech-language pathology—it is the role of the speech-language pathologist to identify children with speech or language impairments and provide speech and language services to help prevent or improve communicative impairments.

THE ROLE OF THE SPECIAL EDUCATION TEACHER

Within each child's IEP is information about the services he is eligible for to help him with his special needs. Usually, but not always, these services involve a special education teacher. Because it is important that each child receive special services in the least restrictive environment, the type, amount of time the services are provided, and location of the provision of services will vary with each child. Sometimes, a resource room or pull-out model is used. In this situation, the special education teacher may take one or more students into her classroom for direct instruction. In early childhood settings, the trend is toward a collaborative model in which the special education teacher collaborates with the general education teacher to provide needed services. The most common collaborative models include the following:

- Lead teacher—In this model, there is a lead teacher, who is often the general education teacher, who provides instruction in a specific subject area. The special education teacher observes the instruction and designs activities for children with special needs. These activities may help ensure that the child understands a concept or provide adaptations and modifications that enable the child to participate in a related task or activity.

- Learning center—In this situation, both teachers (general education and special education) are responsible for instruction in a specific location of the classroom. Often, this method is used in the context of learning centers. Children are assembled into groups that rotate through each center. Special education teachers may deliver instruction in areas that relate to one or more children. This method allows participation by children with diagnosed special needs and may also permit others who just need extra assistance to have access to the instruction. This model also works well when the general education teacher has limited knowledge of special education, as it provides extra assistance to a large number of students.

- Team teaching—In this situation, both teachers work simultaneously to provide instruction. Either teacher with the necessary background knowledge in the subject introduces new concepts and materials to the class. The teachers work as a team to reinforce learning and provide assistance to students as needed. Special education teachers provide specially designed instruction to students with IEPs through direct instruction and modifications of specific content as needed.

- Consultation—This model utilizes the special education teacher as a resource while most of the child's direct instruction is provided by the regular education teacher. The majority of service to a student with an IEP is indirect. The special education teacher provides information to the regular education teacher on how to modify instruction to meet the student's needs.

WORKING WITH PARAPROFESSIONALS AND INSTRUCTIONAL ASSISTANTS

A paraprofessional is someone trained to assist the teacher in the classroom. Your relationship with the paraprofessional is critically important to the success or failure of a child in an inclusive setting. Sometimes parapro-fessionals or instructional assistants work with the child throughout the day to assist her with needs such as toileting, eating, or moving from place to place. Other times a paraprofessional may be assigned to a specific class-room to assist with more than one child. It is very important that you and the paraprofessional work together as a team to help the child make prog-ress and achieve success throughout the school year. If possible, arrange regular meetings with the paraprofessionals in your classroom and ask for their input on issues such as the child's progress and behavior as well as suggestions for adaptations that might help the child complete a particular task. Talk about ways to help the child with things that challenge her. It is also very important that you and the paraprofessional work together to avoid learned helplessness, which occurs when a child with special needs discovers that, if she pretends to be "helpless" and "needy," someone will eventually do things for her that she could easily do for herself. Even chil-dren with severe challenges learn how to act helpless if someone is always there to do everything for them. The ability to function as independently as possible is an important goal for all children with special needs.

TERMS USED IN THIS CHAPTER

assistive technology—any item that supports or helps children with special needs gain greater independence.

behaviorism—belief that learning results in a permanent change in behavior, which is brought about through experience.

constructivism—belief that it is not the environment or an individual activity that facilitates the development of these constructs, but how well the child can mentally process the information that the brain receives.

cueing—a technique that gives the child clues about what he is expected to do.

interdisciplinary model of service delivery—consists of profession-als from different disciplines who plan educational programming for the child.

learned helplessness—occurs when a child with special needs discov-ers that, if she pretends to be helpless and needy, someone will eventu-ally do things for her that she could easily do for herself.

modeling—showing the learner how to do a task.

successive approximation—also referred to as *shaping*. When a child is trying to learn a new activity or work on solving a problem that may be difficult for him, it helps reinforce his efforts when he receives praise for close approximations. This praise or reward helps him keep trying to achieve a new goal.

RESOURCES USED IN THIS CHAPTER

Bruns, D. A., & Mogharreban, C. (2007). The gap between beliefs and practices: Early childhood practitioners' perceptions about inclusion. *Journal of Research in Childhood Education, 21*(3), 229–241.

Driessen, G., Smit, F., & Sleegers, P. (2005). Parental involvement and educational achievement. *British Educational Research Journal, 31*(4), 509–532.

Harnad, S. (1982). Neoconstructivism: A unifying theme for the cognitive sciences. In T. Simon & R. Scholes (Eds.), Language, mind and brain (pp. 1–11). Hillsdale, NJ: Lawrence Erlbaum.

Huitt, W., & Hummel, J. (2006). An overview of the behavioral perspective. *Educational Psychology Interactive* [Electronic version]. Valdosta, GA: Valdosta State University.

Kearsley, G. (1999). *Explorations in learning and instruction: The theory into practice database.* Retrieved September 5, 2007, from http://tip .psychology.org/theories.html

National Association for the Education of Young Children. (2006). *Policy statement on best practice.* Washington, DC: Author.

SUGGESTED READING

DeVore, S., & Russell, K. (2007). Early childhood education and care for children with disabilities: Facilitating inclusive practice [Electronic version]. *Early Childhood Education Journal, 35*(2), 189–198.

Filler, J., & Xu, Y. (2006). Including children with disabilities in early childhood education programs: Individualizing developmentally appropriate practices [Electronic version]. *Childhood Education, 83*(2), 92.

Frankel, E. B. (2004). Supporting inclusive care and education for young children with special needs and their families; an international perspective [Electronic version]. *Childhood Education, 80*(6), 310.

McLeskey, J. (2004). Classic articles in special education articles that shaped the field, 1960 to 1996 [Electronic version]. *Remedial and Special Education, 25*(2), 79–87.

Salmon, M., & Sainato, D. (2005). Beyond Pinocchio: Puppets as teaching tools in inclusive early childhood classrooms [Electronic version]. *Young Exceptional Children, 8*(3), 12–19.

THE RESEARCH SAYS . . .

What Early Childhood Practitioners Think About Inclusion

An exploratory study examined beliefs about inclusion among Head Start and public pre-kindergarten (pre-K) teachers. Using the STARS (Support and Technical Assistance through Relationships and Skill Building) needs assessment, which was developed to learn about inclusion-related beliefs and training needs, researchers from Southern Illinois University conducted research in 14 Head Start and 29 pre-K programs. Their results indicated professionals overwhelmingly believe that all young children benefit from inclusive settings and are more alike than different. However, they found that both groups felt that the strategies and adaptations necessary to assist a child with a disability are not always easy to prepare and implement. The primary training needs for both groups included the following: (1) behavior issues, (2) communication strategies, and (3) assessment. The authors concluded that while professionals generally feel that inclusive practices are important for children with special needs, there is still a need for ongoing support and training for those working with these children.

Bruns, D. A., & Mogharreban, C. (2007). The gap between beliefs and practices: Early childhood practitioners' perceptions about inclusion. *Journal of Research in Childhood Education, 21*(3), 229–241.

Part II

Who Are the Children With Children With Special Needs?

Children With Vision Impairments

3

Figure 3.1   Puzzles with knobs and large pieces help children with visual impairments.

HOW DO YOUNG CHILDREN DEVELOP VISION?

Most parents remember the first time they looked into the eyes of their newborn child and the joy they experienced when the child gazed back at them. From the moment they are born, babies are aware of their surroundings—light sources in particular. As they perceive light, they simply notice the source. As their vision becomes more developed, however, they learn to pay attention to the light source and to focus on what they see. Soon, they are tracking light or following the source of light with their eyes, and they begin to notice nearby objects. Then, as their vision improves, they quickly learn to focus on more distant objects. In addition, their peripheral vision, or side vision, develops before central or front vision. In summary,

- Light is perceived before the awareness of other things.
- Awareness initially causes an infant to notice the surroundings and later to focus on and ultimately recognize people and objects.
- Interest starts in objects nearest the child and is later directed toward more distant objects.
- Peripheral (side vision) develops before central or front vision (seeing what is in front of the child).

WHAT CAUSES VISUAL IMPAIRMENTS IN YOUNG CHILDREN?

According to Foster and Gilbert (1997), the following are the most common causes of severe visual impairments in young children:

- cortical visual impairment (CVI)—eyes develop normally, but damage occurs in the visual cortex of the brain. Limitations in vision can range from mild to severe. In severe cases, the child has no light perception at all.
- retinopathy of prematurity (ROP)—a condition resulting in vision loss that can develop in infants who are born prematurely.
- optic nerve hypoplasia—underdeveloped optic nerve tissue, which may result in damage to one or both eyes. This is a congenital condition that occurs in the womb.
- microphthalmia—a congenital condition that results in very small, poorly formed eyes. The size and malformations in the eyes result in very poor vision.
- anomphthalmia—a very rare condition in which the child is born without an eyeball in one or both eyes.
- glaucoma—increased pressure in the eye that damages the optic nerve and ultimately leads to potential loss of peripheral vision and blindness. This condition can be successfully treated if found early enough.
- reintoblastoma—cancer of the eye that can result in severe vision impairment.
- congenital cataracts—a condition in which the lens of the eyes becomes clouded. This condition can be corrected with surgery.

HOW ARE VISION IMPAIRMENTS CLASSIFIED?

The term *visual impairment*, or visual loss, does not specify the eye disorder or condition that caused the problem. Rather, it is a term used to describe the functional or residual vision available to the child. Determination of the degree of a child's functional vision or vision loss is usually made by an optometrist and/or an ophthalmologist. In some cases, the child may have been diagnosed by a pediatric ophthalmologist, a doctor specializing in diagnosis and treatment of eye disease in young children. Four categories of visual impairment are normally used to describe a child's residual or functional vision: partially sighted, low vision, legally blind, or totally blind.

1. Partially sighted means that there are some mild visual problems, but, with special adaptations and appropriate light, the child can function in the general education classroom.
2. Low vision is used to describe a child with a severely reduced field of vision, resulting in reduced visual acuity or reduced ability to see normal or necessary contrast between objects. A child with low vision may have one or more of the following issues: difficulty recognizing faces; difficulty seeing detail in printed materials; or problems distinguishing steps, curbs, or uneven surfaces from flat surfaces.
3. Legally blind indicates that a child has less than 20/200 vision in the better eye or a very limited field of vision (20 degrees at its widest point).
4. Totally blind indicates a complete or almost complete absence of vision. Totally blind students learn via Braille or other nonvisual media and have very little, if any, residual vision. A person who is totally blind may or may not be able to perceive the presence of light.

WHAT RESOURCES ARE AVAILABLE TO HELP THE CHILD FUNCTION IN MY CLASSROOM?

Depending on the type and severity of the vision loss, the child may require the services of an educational vision specialist, who may be either a teacher certified to work with children who are blind or an orientation and mobility specialist concerned with issues such as

*   assessing the child's functional or useful vision;
*   training the child to use his functional vision in everyday situations;

- training the child and/or the classroom teacher to use an optical device for magnification; and
- coordinating the specialists working with the child, including family members and teachers.

By the time a child arrives in your classroom, he will probably have already received a functional vision assessment. This evaluation helps determine how much usable vision a child has, and how it will affect his ability to participate in daily routines. This evaluation is usually given after the child has been diagnosed by an ophthalmologist or optometrist. Usually, a new functional vision assessment is conducted every three years. This functional vision assessment combines the information from the medical report with information about how well the child can see objects, both near and distant, how well the child can function in a typical setting, and recommendations for educational programming and classroom observations (Pogrund & Fazzi, 2002).

HOW DO CHILDREN WITH VISION IMPAIRMENTS LEARN?

Children who are blind or visually impaired need to learn specialized skills in order to function independently at home and at school. In order to obtain information and understand what is going on around them, children with visual impairments depend on verbal cues and other adaptations to help them learn. Specially trained teachers, such as teachers of the visually impaired and orientation and mobility specialists can help you understand the importance of verbal influence and can assist in making necessary adaptations for these children in your classroom. The following list describes some of the specialized skills that visually impaired children may need:

- technology—depending on the type and severity of the loss, adaptive technologies, such as a lighted magnification device, might be useful.
- computer skills—many computer games and programs have been adapted for blind or visually impaired people.
- early literacy skills—a child may need printed materials that contain large print.
- residual vision training—children with visual impairments often need the opportunity to learn how to use their available vision to their advantage.

- safety and environmental training—this includes using methods that allow children with visual impairments to orient themselves to new environments and may include mobility tools such as long canes (for object detection when walking) or using seeing-eye dogs.
- social skills—learning how to be a friend and have a friend. Children who are able to involve themselves with other children learn to read the body language of others for social cues. Children with visual impairments need to learn alternative ways to know what to do in social situations (such as verbal cues, etc.). More discussion about adapting to social environments can be found later in this chapter.
- functional skills—these are the skills that the child will use throughout her life, such as dressing, eating, toileting, and bathing.

PREPARING THE EARLY CHILDHOOD ENVIRONMENT

The curriculum for children with vision impairments must emphasize concrete learning. Because the child with visual impairments depends on his other senses for clues about the environment, it is important to provide opportunities for learning by encouraging him to listen to and identify sounds and explore his surroundings through touch. Additionally, you can make it easier for the child to know about his environment and what is happening around him by always using clear and concise verbal directions. Use the child's name, and, when necessary, touch the child on the arm or shoulder to get his attention. This will cue the child that you are speaking to him specifically, and not to the entire group. Remember to ask the child questions that determine whether he understood what you were describing.

SUGGESTIONS FOR CHILDREN WITH LOW VISION

While the classroom environment should be visually stimulating for all children, those with low vision will benefit from pictures, posters, and printed materials that include large, distinct, and colorful objects, rather than those with more intricate details. Although a well-lighted classroom is critically important for a child with low vision, direct sunlight is not recommended because it can cause glare and, in some cases, the bright light is painful for the child. In addition, be aware that some surfaces, such as "white boards" and other smooth surfaces, can cause unnecessary glare that may result in the child being unable to use her residual vision.

Also, keep in mind that the outdoor environment can be very dangerous for a child with visual impairments. It is very important for the teacher to inspect the outdoor play area for things that a child with visual impairments may not see clearly, such as a ball or discarded toy that might cause her to stumble or trip.

Much of your instruction for the preschool child with vision impairments will involve instruction in three areas: training in visual perception, facilitating early literacy skills, and developing social skills.

1. Training in visual perception—children with functional residual vision must be taught to use it as efficiently as possible. This includes being able to use their residual vision for such things as

- developing figure-ground discrimination;
- understanding shape consistency;
- recognizing printed materials; and
- using visual aids, such as magnifiers.

2. Early literacy skills—reading to children can help build early literacy skills, which are critical for later success in reading. For most children, an important part of the experience is the combination of seeing pictures and hearing the text being read. However, children with visual impairments may not be able to see clearly the pictures shown to the rest of the class. In this situation, providing the child with a low vision copy of the book, or having a copy of the book mounted on a table-top easel, is often effective. It is still important to note that pictures with too much detail will be very confusing for most children with low vision.

3. Developing social skills—as was briefly discussed earlier, children learn to interact with each other by depending on visual cues to tell them what to do. It is very difficult for a child with visual impairments to interact with peers, because he is often unable to watch other children and imitate how they interact with each other. In addition, visual cues, such as how the other children are playing or what they are playing with, may not be available for a child with a visual impairment. To help the child successfully socialize with his peers, the teacher will need to facilitate opportunities for positive interactions to occur. For example, a teacher might do the following:

- Set up opportunities for the child with visual impairments to interact with a peer or small group.
- Give the child opportunities to explore specific areas of the classroom when other children are not present. This helps the

child orient herself to the specific area in which an interaction might take place.

- Describe anticipated situations for the child so that he knows how he can best participate. For example, you might use a phrase like, "Adrian, Marisa is handing you a block. She is in front of you." As the child reaches forth, the teacher could say, "Marisa, place the block in Adrian's hand."

- Provide encouraging feedback when a child does interact well with others in a small group or play situation.

- Remind peers that the child with vision impairments (especially

Figure 3.2   Children with visual impairments rely on touch for environmental cues.

significant vision impairments) uses touch to help "see" things. Explain that the child might use a "soft touch" to explore someone's face or a new toy or item in the classroom.

SUGGESTIONS FOR CHILDREN WHO ARE BLIND OR SEVERELY VISION IMPAIRED

Children who are blind or severely vision impaired will require the help and expertise of either an orientation and mobility specialist or a certified teacher of the visually impaired. They will be trained in how to use devices that are common to people who are blind, such as Braille, and in the use of mobility devices, such as a cane. In the past, canes were often not introduced until a child was older, perhaps at age nine or ten. However, more recent research has shown that canes and "pre-cane" training should begin much earlier. Some children in preschool classrooms are already receiving training in how to use a cane for mobility.

The use of service animals, such as seeing-eye dogs, is rare among very young children. A specialist can help you determine the need for specific adaptations for children who are blind. The following are guidelines that may be followed when leading a young child who is blind. Note that some of these differ from the guidelines for leading older people.

1. Approach the child and call her by name.
2. Hold out your arm and invite the child to hold your wrist.
3. Walk slightly in front of the child, keeping in mind that your steps might be longer and wider than hers.
4. Talk about where you are going, using simple, descriptive sentences.
5. When helping a child sit down in a chair, take her hand and place it on the back of the chair.
6. When going up or down steps, pause and say "step up" or "step down." When you reach level ground, take a step, then pause to give the child time to complete the last step. Remind the child that you will stop at the edge of each step and wait for her to step up or down, before going to the next step.

SUMMARY

Children with vision impairments:

1. Depend on touch and sound to help them learn new concepts. Some children will touch a person's face as a way to "see" what he or she looks like.
2. Will need help in learning to use their other senses for clues about the environment.
3. Benefit from your description of things and from having the opportunity to explore things by examining them with the other senses.
4. Can benefit from line drawings with a minimum of background clutter. For example, use a simple line drawing of a horse, rather than a farm scene with a barn and many animals.
5. Should receive preferential seating during routine classroom activities. If the child has peripheral vision, make sure he is seated so that peripheral vision is optimized. Lighting should be appropriate and not cause a "glare" effect.
6. Benefit from a safe environment that is free of obstacles that the child could trip over.

TERMS USED IN THIS CHAPTER

functional vision assessment—an evaluation that helps determine how much usable vision a child has and how it will affect her ability to go about daily routines.

orientation and mobility specialist—specially trained teachers who can help you understand the importance of verbal influences and can assist in making necessary adaptations for these children in your classroom.

pediatric ophthalmologist—a doctor who specializes in the diagnosis and treatment of eye disease in young children.

peripheral vision—the ability to see objects and movement outside of the direct line of vision.

RESOURCES USED IN THIS CHAPTER

Celeste, M. (2006). Play behaviors and social interactions of a child who is blind: In theory and practice. *Journal of Visual Impairment & Blindness, 100*(2), 75–90.

Foster, A., & Gilbert, C. (1997). Epidemiology of visual impairment in children. In D. Taylor (Ed.), *Pediatric ophthalmology* (2nd ed.). pp. 3–12. Oxford, UK: Blackwell Science.

Pogrund, R. L., & Fazzi, D. L. (Eds). (2002). *Early focus: Working with children who are blind or visually impaired and their families.* New York: American Federation for the Blind Press.

SUGGESTED READING

Celeste, M. (2006). Play behaviors and social interactions of a child who is blind: In theory and practice. *Journal of Visual Impairment & Blindness, 100*(2), 75–90.

Hatton, D. D., Bailey, D. B., Burchinal, M. R., & Ferrell, K. A. (1997). Development growth curves of preschool children with vision impairments. *Child Development, 68*(5), 788–806.

Hatton, D., Catlett, C., Winton, P. J., & Mitchell, A. (2002). Resources within reason: Resources for working with infants, toddlers, and young children who are blind or visually impaired. *Young Exceptional Children, 5*(4), 28.

Holbrook, M. C., & Koenig, A. J. (Eds.). (2000). *Foundations of education, volume I: History and theory of teaching children and youths with visual impairments* (2nd ed.). Sewickley, PA: American Federation for the Blind Press.

Mendiola, R., Bahar, C., Brody, J., & Slott, G. L. (2005). *A unique way of learning: Teaching young children with optic nerve hypoplasia.* Los Angeles: Blind Children's Center.

THE RESEARCH SAYS . . .

Play Behaviors in Young Children Who Are Blind

The author examined play behaviors and the social interactions generated by a preschool child with blindness using a case study approach. The participant in the study was functioning at or above grade level on all her developmental milestones. However, after observation across time, the researcher found that the young girl demonstrated very limited play behaviors and significant issues with social competence and peer interactions. Past research has found that children with vision impairments demonstrate play behaviors that are primarily exploratory in nature. The author provides some implications for the field based on this research. Those implications include the following: a need to continually access both play behaviors and social interaction skills of children who are visually impaired; development of additional strategies that support the social competence of children with vision loss; helping children with vision impairments develop a social repertoire of skills in the area of social development; and training teachers and professionals to know how to help children develop the social skills necessary to have sustained positive social interactions with peers. The author concludes that simply placing children with vision impairments in inclusive environments is not enough to enable them to be successful. In addition, it is critically important that educators identify and help students develop the social skills necessary for successful interactions with peers.

Celeste, M. (2006). Play behaviors and social interactions of a child who is blind: In theory and practice. *Journal of Visual Impairment & Blindness, 100*(2), 75–90.

Children With Hearing Loss

4

Figure 4.1   Children with hearing loss interact best when they can see the face of their playmate.

DEFINING HEARING LOSS

A child's hearing loss is generally defined as either congenital or acquired. A congenital hearing loss is caused by factors that occur before or during birth. Examples include a hearing loss caused by exposure to chemicals or trauma in the womb. An acquired hearing loss occurs after a child's birth and may be the result of a specific disease or an injury. The most common acquired hearing losses in children include:

- ear infections, such as otitis media. While otitis media can be cured with medication, if left untreated, it can cause permanent hearing loss.
- medications that damage the ear.
- meningitis with accompanying high fever.
- common childhood diseases, such as measles, chicken pox, flu, or mumps.
- encephalitis (inflammation of the brain).

- head trauma or injury, such as a blow to the head.
- consistent exposure to loud noises.

Many states have laws requiring that newborns receive a newborn screening test to help determine at birth if they have a hearing impairment. Most preschools and all public schools routinely screen children for hearing problems. A preschool child may receive a hearing screening by a nurse or other health care professional. Because young children are prone to ear infections and often have allergies or other temporary conditions that may affect hearing, screening exams are sometimes repeated before the child is referred to a specialist for formal testing. After a second screening, if the child still does not hear sounds at specific noise levels, the child will be referred to a specialist, such as an audiologist (a specialist who works with children with hearing loss) or otolaryngologist (a doctor who specializes in the ear, nose, and throat). It is important not to assume that failing to pass a routine hearing screening indicates that the child has a permanent hearing loss. Ear infections are very common in young children and will affect the outcome of a hearing screening. An audiologist will give the child a series of tests to determine the extent of the child's hearing loss. The most common test is performed using an audiometer that produces an audiogram (a chart or graph), which provides detailed information about the child's ability to hear. Based on the audiogram, a professional can tell whether the child has a hearing loss and, if so, determine how serious it is.

WHAT DETERMINES THE DEGREE OF HEARING LOSS?

Hearing losses are usually defined as mild, moderate, severe, or profound, depending on the child's ability to hear certain sounds at various frequencies. A hearing threshold of between 0 and 25 decibels (dB) is considered normal.

- Mild hearing loss indicates the softest sounds that can be heard with the better ear are between 25 and 40 dB. Children with mild hearing loss have some difficulty keeping up with conversations, especially in noisy surroundings such as in a busy classroom or the cafeteria.
- Moderate hearing loss indicates the softest sounds that can be heard with the better ear are between 40 and 70 dB. Those who suffer from moderate hearing loss have difficulty understanding normal conversations and may require the use of a hearing aid or other special amplification device.

- Severe hearing loss indicates the softest sounds that can be heard with the better ear are between 70 and 95 dB. People who suffer from severe hearing loss will benefit from powerful hearing aids. However, they still must rely heavily on lip-reading even when they use hearing aids. Some people with severe hearing loss will also use sign language.
- Profound hearing loss, referred to as deafness, indicates that the softest sounds that can be heard with the better ear are from 95 dB or more. People who suffer from profound hearing loss must rely on lip-reading and/or sign language to communicate.

SO, WHAT ABOUT HEARING AIDS?

Children with certain types of hearing loss will benefit from the use of an amplification device. The most common amplification device is a hearing aid, which is usually prescribed by an audiologist or otolaryngologist. Research has shown that the earlier a child receives a hearing aid, the better his overall prognosis. Many audiology clinics have loaner programs that loan a hearing aid to a child with some hearing loss so that families and caregivers are able to determine its effectiveness before purchase. This also helps by indicating whether that particular type of hearing aid is appropriate for the child and whether the child can tolerate wearing the hearing aid. If a child in your class wears a hearing aid, his speech pathologist or audiologist can give you basic instructions as to its use and maintenance, such as when and how to change the battery, and how to set the volume at a level that is appropriate for the child.

COCHLEAR IMPLANT

A cochlear implant is an electronic device that helps provide a beneficial level of sound to a person who is profoundly deaf or severely hard-of-hearing. The implant is surgically implanted under the skin. The device has a small microphone to pick up sound from the surrounding environment, as well as a speech processing device that arranges or decodes sounds that are enhanced by the microphone. A transmitter receives signals from the speech processor and converts them to electric impulses, which are sent to various regions along the auditory nerve. The result is that the implant provides a useful representation of sound, which in turn helps the user understand speech. It does not restore normal hearing; it improves how the person with the implant is able to hear and distinguish sounds. Cochlear implants have been given to children as young as two years of age, and, in most cases, can improve the child's chances for oral language development and help her learn to communicate more effectively. However, not all types of hearing loss respond to a cochlear implant and only a professional can help the child's family determine if having an implant will be beneficial (Tomblin, Spencer, Flock, Tyler, & Gantz, 1999).

HOW WILL HEARING LOSS AFFECT CHILDREN IN MY CLASSROOM?

According to the American Speech Hearing-Language Association, hearing loss can affect young children in four major areas:

1. It causes delays in the development of communication skills, specifically, how well children understand speech (receptive language) and how well children are able to use language skills (expressive language).
2. Because a child with a hearing impairment usually has a language or communication problem, he may not progress academically as fast as his peers. Reduced academic achievement is not a result of the child's being less intelligent than his peers; rather, it is due to the fact that almost all activities in a preschool setting are based on using language. If a child cannot hear language or interpret it clearly, it is very difficult for him to use it appropriately.
3. Since most children with hearing loss also have difficulties with communication, it is difficult for them to talk to and interact with peers. Children may feel socially isolated, and, as a result, may have poor self-esteem.
4. It may influence future vocational choices.

SOCIAL ISOLATION

As has been mentioned, a child with hearing loss may feel socially isolated and have difficulty making friends. However, steps can be taken to include the child in activities with her peers, which will help add to her sense of fitting in and belonging. For example, cooperative learning in a small-group activity is a meaningful way to engage all members of the classroom and promote positive social interactions. As children work together to achieve a common goal, the child with a hearing impairment will feel more confident in herself. The following are suggestions for organizing group work in the classroom:

1. Keep groups small to prompt conversation and interaction.
2. Seat students at round tables where all faces are visible (Oral Deaf Education, 2005).
3. Make use of visual and/or tactile resources, so that a child with a hearing impairment can gather clues from the surrounding environment, and ultimately become more fully involved in the activity.
4. Assign roles to group members, such as speaker, artist, materials monitor, etc., so that each student will have the chance to participate—you may want to practice using these roles before expecting students to do so on their own.
5. Reinforce positive interactions as they occur during group work time.

COMMUNICATING IN THE CLASSROOM

Communication is very important for children. As has been discussed, those without adequate functional hearing often miss opportunities for positive interactions with peers, due to the difficulty they often have in communicating with others. Because effective communication is the cornerstone to attaining both social and academic skills, it is imperative that the child with hearing loss be able to communicate as clearly as possible, and, in ways that can be understood by others. Depending on the type and severity of the loss, to enable a child to more effectively interact through communication with his peers, one of the following approaches may be used:

1. Auditory-oral—this approach attempts to utilize the residual or remaining hearing that a child has. If the child wears a hearing aid or has received a cochlear implant, this is the approach that will likely be most successful. Children are taught techniques, such as speech-reading (lip reading), to help supplement the information that their residual hearing does not supply for them, as well as specific techniques for listening and speaking. This method does not employ the use of sign language.

2. Auditory-verbal—similar to the auditory-oral approach, this method helps children make use of residual hearing, but, in this approach,

it is usually achieved through the use of a hearing aid or cochlear implant. This method relies very heavily on the child's ability to rely only on listening skills, since it does not include the use of speech reading (lip reading) or sign language.

3. Cued speech—this method relies on the child's ability to learn to both "see" and "hear" spoken language. The primary focus of this system is to help the child watch for movements that the mouth makes when someone talks. It combines (a) eight hand shapes (called cues), which indicate groups of consonants, and (b) four positions around the face, which indicate vowel sounds. Because lip movements used in making certain sounds can be seen on the lips but often look alike (such as "b" and "p"), and because other lip movements cannot be seen on the lips (such as "k"), the hand cues help the child tell what sounds are being voiced.

Figure 4.2   Some children with hearing loss depend on sign language to communicate [Thank You]. *Illustration by Justin Mitchel*

4. Sign language—This is traditionally used by those children with the most severe hearing loss or by children who have limited residual hearing. The two types of sign language most commonly used are Signed Exact English (SEE) and American Sign Language (ASL). Signed Exact English follows the grammatical structure of the English language, but, in many ways, it is almost like learning a completely separate language. American Sign Language uses signs to represent *concepts* rather than following a strict grammatical construct.

5. Total communication—This approach combines a variety of methods to help the child communicate as effectively as possible and will usually utilize one or more of the following: sign language, finger spelling, speech reading, speaking, and, when applicable, the use of hearing aids or a cochlear implant.

EFFECTS OF HEARING LOSS ON
SPEECH (ORAL LANGUAGE)

For children with hearing impairments who are oral (have the ability to speak), speaking clearly or understandably is often difficult or impossible. This is because children with hearing loss usually cannot hear soft speech sounds, including words (or sounds) that include, "s," "sh," "f," "t," and "k." Because of the difficulty in hearing such sounds, a child may say something that sounds like "wan-oo-ee," when she is actually trying to say, "want cookie." Since a child with severe hearing loss cannot hear her own voice when she speaks, her speech may seem too loud and often the pitch is higher than normal. In addition, the child usually has considerable difficulty with sentence structure. Since they know fewer words than their peers, their sentences are often shorter and simpler. Additional problems arise when the child learns rules of grammar and writing sentences. As they get older, children with hearing loss generally have problems with such constructs as verb tense, possessives, and word endings, like 's' and 'ed.'

REDUCED ACADEMIC ACHIEVEMENT

Reading and math concepts will be especially difficult for children with hearing loss. In general, those with mild to moderate hearing loss will often perform much more poorly than their peers in these areas. In some cases, they will perform academically at a level somewhere between one and four grade levels below their peers; this trend continues as the child gets older. For children with severe to profound hearing loss, the gap between their achievement and that of their peers is even greater. However, research shows that for children who receive early intervention and support, this gap can be much smaller (Martineau, Lamarche, Marcoux, & Bernard, 2001). In addition, parent involvement and quality early learning experiences can play a significant role in improving achievement as the child matures.

SUGGESTIONS FOR THE CLASSROOM

1. When learning new concepts, help the child learn to use all his senses, especially sight.
2. Picture cards are a useful tool to help the child know what to do first, second, third, etc. They also provide additional clues about what the child is expected to do.

3. Seat the child where she can see your face; glare from lights or windows can obstruct the child's view of the teacher's face and make it more difficult for her to see what is said.
4. Use questions and gestures to make sure the child knows what you are asking him to do. It is not uncommon for children with hearing impairments to smile and nod their head as if they understand what is being said, when, in reality, they have no idea what was just said to them.
5. If the child depends on sign language as a method of communication, teach the class a few signs as well.
6. Children with low-frequency hearing loss will have difficulty understanding speech, because most speech sounds occur in low frequencies; look for opportunities to determine what the child can hear.

TERMS USED IN THIS CHAPTER

acquired hearing loss—a condition, such as a hearing loss, that occurs after birth.

audiogram—the chart or graph that displays hearing test results.

audiologist—a specialist who works with children with hearing loss.

audiometer—the machine used to test a person's hearing.

cochlear implant—an electronic device that helps provide a beneficial level of sound to a person who is profoundly deaf or severely hard-of-hearing.

congenital—a condition, such as a hearing loss, that is present at or before birth.

encephalitis—an inflammation of the brain.

otitis media—a type of ear infection where fluid builds up behind the ear drum. It is curable, if treated with antibiotics, but it can result in permanent hearing loss if left untreated.

otolaryngologist—a doctor who specializes in the ear, nose, and throat.

RESOURCES USED IN THIS CHAPTER

Lenden, J. M., & Flipsen, P. (2007). Prosody and voice characteristics of children with cochlear implants. *Journal of Communication Disorders, 40*(1), 66–81.

Martineau, G., Lamarche, P., Marcoux, S., & Bernard, P. (2001). The effect of early intervention on academic achievement. *Early Education and Development, 12*(2), 75–89.

Oral Deaf Education. (2005). *Oral deaf education library—Frequently asked questions.* Retrieved August 7, 2007, from http://www.oraldeafed .org/library/faq.org

Tomblin, J. B., Spencer, L., Flock, S., Tyler, R., & Gantz, B. (1999). A comparison of language achievement in children with cochlear implants and children using hearing aids. *Journal of Speech, Language, and Hearing Research, 42,* 496–511.

SUGGESTED READING

Humphrey, J. H., & Alcorn, B. J. (2001). *So you want to be an interpreter? An introduction to sign language interpreting* (3rd ed.). Amarillo, TX: H&H.

Inglehart, F. (2004). Speech perception by students with cochlear implants using sound-field systems in classrooms. *American Journal of Audiology, 13,* 62–72.

Kluwin, T., Stinson, M., & Colarossi, G. (2002). Social processes and outcomes of in-school contact between deaf and hearing peers. *Journal of Deaf Studies and Deaf Education, 7*(3), 200–213.

Knoors, H., Meuleman, J., & Klatter-Folmer, J. (2003). Parents' and teachers' evaluations of the communicative abilities of deaf children. *American Annals of the Deaf, 148,* 287–294.

Pakulski, L. A., & Kaderavek, J. N. (2002). Children with minimal hearing loss: Interventions in the classroom. *Intervention in School & Clinic, 38*(2), 96–103.

Tharpe, A. M., Ashmead, D. H., & Rothpletz, A. M. (2002). Visual attention in children with normal hearing, children with hearing aids, and children with cochlear implants. *Journal of Speech, Language, and Hearing Research, 45,* 403–413.

THE RESEARCH SAYS . . .

Cochlear Implants Can Result in Better Prosody

The authors looked at young children across time who had cochlear implants. The result was a descriptive, longitudinal study that analyzed the prosody (stress and intonation of everyday speech) and voice characteristics of conversational speech produced by six young children with severe to profound hearing impairments who had been fitted with cochlear implants. A total of 40 samples were analyzed using the following assessment tools: Prosody–Voice Screening Profile (PVSP; Shriberg, L. D., Kwiatkowski, J., & Rasmussen, C. (1990). *Prosody–Voice Screening Profile (PVSP)*. Tuscon, AZ: Communication Skill Builders). The most noticeable problems were with stress (how they emphasized certain syllables) and resonance quality. Some difficulties were noted with rate of speech, loudness, and laryngeal quality, but there were no consistent difficulties with phrasing or pitch. This suggested that prosody and voice characteristics in this population are different from those typically observed in children with severe to profound hearing impairments. The authors feel that these findings suggest that cochlear implants offer some significant benefits to children with hearing impairment in terms of prosody and voice outcomes.

Lenden, J. M., & Flipsen, P. (2007). Prosody and voice characteristics of children with cochlear implants. *Journal of Communication Disorders, 40*(1), 66–81.

Children With Cognitive Challenges

5

Figure 5.1   Children with cognitive challenges often respond to tactile stimulation.

UNDERSTANDING THE CHALLENGES FOR CHILDREN WITH COGNITIVE DELAYS

Children with cognitive challenges face many more difficulties learning new concepts than their peers. How much they learn and how well they develop often depends on more than just the level of their cognitive challenges. It can depend on factors such as:

- How well they get along with others;
- Whether they adjust well to new surroundings and changes in the daily routine;

- How motivated they are to try new things; and
- Other coexisting disabilities, such as motor impairments, speech and language delays, and behavior or emotional issues.

Generally, when we think of a child with cognitive challenges, the word mental retardation comes to mind. Mental retardation (also called developmental delay or cognitive delay) is a term that means much more than just having an intelligence quotient (IQ) below 70. It generally refers to a pattern of learning that is slower than that of children who are developing according to traditional milestones. This slower pattern of learning may be in areas of development such as basic motor skills, speech and language skills, self-help skills, or problem-solving skills. To be classified as mentally retarded, the slow development must occur in childhood and persist into adulthood. While cognitive delays are not curable, a student's strengths and skills can be maximized with careful planning and early intervention. One thing is certain: Research clearly indicates that the sooner a child with cognitive challenges receives early intervention, the better the outcome for future success is likely to be (Hebbeler et al., 2007).

CHARACTERISTICS OF CHILDREN WITH COGNITIVE CHALLENGES

Children with cognitive delays or challenges will develop more slowly than their peers do. It will take them longer to learn a new skill, or they may forget a skill that was previously learned. In addition, their attention span will be much shorter than that of their peers. Language and communication skills are often very difficult for a child with cognitive challenges. In general, they learn fewer words than their peers, and they speak in much shorter sentences. For example, a five-year-old usually speaks in complete sentences with at least one descriptive word, as in, "Look at that cool red truck." Whereas, a child with a cognitive challenge looking at the same red truck might say, "Car go."

It is very challenging for children with cognitive challenges to process new information; they will also have problems transferring a learned skill to a new setting. In other words, they do not generalize information readily. For this reason, a child with cognitive challenges will need the following:

- new information broken down into smaller steps
- more opportunities to practice a new skill

- frequent reviews of previously learned skills, especially after vacation or holiday time when they have been out of school
- cues, such as picture sequence cards, to help them remember the steps in performing a task or skill

However, given time, practice, and support, children with cognitive challenges can and do learn.

EDUCATIONAL IMPLICATIONS

Children with mild cognitive delays may not be diagnosed until they begin kindergarten or first grade. Many professionals are hesitant to diagnose a child with a cognitive delay if they feel the delay may only be the result of a developmental lag, and, given time and experiences, the child could develop normally. For this reason, many young children with cognitive delays are labeled developmentally delayed until they reach first or second grade.

Obviously, the more severe a child's intellectual delay, the more difficult it will be for her to learn; children with severe cognitive delays are usually labeled as such by the time they are three. For some children, especially those with more significant delays, goals are less academic and focus on how to be independent in daily routines. Their goals may include learning skills like feeding themselves, toileting, and dressing without assistance. Regardless of the degree and severity of the cognitive challenge, many children in early childhood settings will need help in learning functional skills.

Figure 5.2 Teach functional skills, such as handwashing.

WHAT ARE FUNCTIONAL SKILLS AND WHY ARE THEY IMPORTANT?

Functional skills have been given many names: self-help skills, everyday skills, independent living skills, and daily life skills. Regardless of which term is used, these activities are the skills that children will use throughout their lives to carry out simple tasks such as washing, bathing, eating, and dressing. These skills will help them function independently in daily routines just like their peers. Functional skills also include learning survival words or words that are used frequently in daily life such as restroom, exit, on, off, and stop.

In addition to helping the child gain independence, functional skills make him feel more in control of his world. Predictability and routines are very important to children with cognitive challenges. Taking care of their personal needs provides the child with the daily life skills he will use throughout his lifetime. Most important, learning basic functional skills helps the child's self-esteem, by giving him a sense of accomplishment and the confidence that comes from doing it "all by himself." In other words, because of the delay in their development, many children with cognitive challenges will enter preschool or kindergarten unable to do everyday things independently.

HOW DO I TEACH EVERYDAY TASKS (FUNCTIONAL SKILLS)?

The first step is to determine what everyday tasks you wish to teach, keeping in mind that success often depends on both the child's developmental level as well as the family's willingness to help her practice her new skill at home. Working with the child's family to help determine what life skills to teach first facilitates working together as a team. If the skill is a high priority for the child's family, they are more likely to work with her at home to practice and learn it. When teaching any skill, it is also important that you and the child's family use the same method of instruction. You must each use the same words, phrases, and picture cues to encourage the child. Multiple opportunities to practice a new skill will help the child learn the skill.

It is also important that functional skills be taught as well as practiced in the context of daily routines and in the environment in which that skill would likely happen. For example, you would not want to teach a child to wash his hands while sitting at a table in your classroom. Instead, you would take him to the natural environment, in this case the sink, where washing his hands would normally occur. Likewise, you would not try to teach him the steps to dressing himself during large group time. These types of artificial practice are not only a waste of time, but are also very confusing for the child. Later, as the child gets older, he will need to learn other functional skills, such as telling time, using money, and preparing simple snacks. However, during his preschool and kindergarten years, functional skills generally are divided into the following categories:

- eating
  - using utensils to feed yourself
  - understanding basic table rules
  - utilizing mealtime as an opportunity for social interaction
- bathroom skills
  - asking to go to the bathroom
  - taking care of own toilet needs without assistance
  - washing hands after toileting
  - handling unplanned situations such as accidents
- personal hygiene
  - brushing teeth after meals
  - washing and drying face
  - washing hands and maintaining a clean appearance
- dressing
  - getting dressed for school
  - getting dressed to go outside
  - taking off clothes
  - putting on shoes
- simple routines
  - getting up in the morning
  - arriving at school
  - learning the daily routine
  - getting ready to go to lunch
  - getting ready to go home
  - adjusting to school routines after a period of being out of school (after vacation, illness, etc.)

WHAT DO I DO FIRST, BEFORE TEACHING A NEW SKILL?

Deciding which skill to teach first involves getting input from a variety of sources, including the child's family and others who work with her, such as the speech pathologist, occupational therapist, or physical therapist. Depending on the developmental level of the child, and whether or not she has motor impairments as well, toileting and feeding herself are usually priority skills for a young child. When planning to teach any new skill, you should follow these general guidelines:

1. Begin by deciding which skill is the most important to the child and his family. This decision should be based on the developmental level of the child and on the wishes of his family. It should also be based on your careful observation of the child. Trying to teach a life skill before the child is developmentally ready can be confusing, frustrating, and frightening for the child; it could result in a delay in him learning the skill.

2. Once you have determined which skill will be taught first, inform everyone who will be working with the child, so all are aware that the plan is to teach something new. Don't forget to include others who work with the child, including your teaching assistant, the child's afterschool caregiver, and other people with whom the child spends a significant amount of time.

3. Make a list of the vocabulary associated with the new skill. Be sure to check with the child's family, so you are both using the same words and the same procedure for practicing the new skill.

4. Make a task analysis or step-by-step guide for completing the skill. Write down each step and go over the list again to see if you have left off anything important.

5. This task analysis will be your guidebook as you teach the child each step in the sequence necessary to master her new skill.

6. Make another, less detailed, task analysis that you will use with the child. This guide is much simpler than the one you made for yourself. Be very specific, concise, and clear about what the child is to do. Use pictures, whenever possible, as they will show the child what to do and serve as a reminder should the child forget an important step.

7. Practice the skill several times yourself using the list you have made for the child. If possible, invite another adult to watch you as you model each step. Remember, things that seem natural to you, like hanging up a towel after you use it or flushing a toilet, are not necessarily natural for the child.

8. Decide on the best time to begin implementation of the new skill. Even if the child is not ready to do the complete task alone, she still may be ready to start learning some of the basic steps.

9. Make sequence cards for each step and use clear pictures. Make another set of cards to send home. It is always good to make a third set of cards as a backup, in case something happens to the sequence cards. Whenever possible, save a copy on the computer for future use.

10. Practice any new skill in the natural environment in which it would occur. For example, tooth brushing should be practiced at a real sink in the bathroom, not at a "pretend" sink, and feeding skills should be learned when the child is eating.

11. Place the sequence cards in front of the child and talk about each one. Remember to use clear, concrete language. Next, model each step for the child before asking him to start the task.

12. Don't forget the home-school connection. Keep the family involved, so that what is learned at school can be reinforced at home.

13. Generalization is often very difficult. Do not be discouraged if a skill that the child has learned at school does not immediately transfer to another environment.

14. Give the child time to practice one step of the skill before going on to the next. Expecting too much, too soon, can be overwhelming for both you and the child.

HOW EXACTLY DOES THIS ALL FIT TOGETHER?

Now that we have some ideas about learning self-help skills, let's look at an example of a specific skill, such as hand-washing. Danielle is a four-year-old in Brenda's classroom. She is developmentally delayed and functions at a level about two years below that of her peers. She enjoys going to the sink and will hold her hands under the water, but Brenda has noticed that often, Danielle just splashes the water around and expects someone to dry her hands for her. Brenda meets with Danielle's family, including her aunt Darla who takes care of her after school. Together, they determine that Danielle's learning to wash her hands independently is a skill that is important to the family and decide that she should learn to wash her hands. Brenda discusses with them the challenges that are specific to Danielle. She also points out that Danielle enjoys mealtime and snack time. Next, Brenda and Darla make a list of the words they will use when teaching Danielle to wash her hands.

Words to use when teaching Danielle to wash her hands:

sink	inside
water	outside
soap	under
rinse	wet
on	dry
off	hot
stop	cold

After reviewing the word list, her teachers decide that Danielle will need to review the concepts of *hot, cold, on,* and *off* before they start teaching her the steps she needs to perform to wash her hands independently. Next, they list the steps they expect Danielle will need to learn to master the task. The following is their list, or task analysis:

Objective: Danielle will wash and dry her hands independently.

1. Walk to the sink.
2. Turn on the water (hot and cold).
3. Run the water over your hands.
4. Pump soap one time and put some soap in your hands (Danielle's family uses liquid soap in a pump bottle).
5. Rub your hands together while singing a song or nursery rhyme such as *Hickory, Dickery, Dock.*
6. Rinse your hands under water—remember to wash off all the soap.
7. Turn off the water.
8. Reach for paper towels to dry your hands.
9. Dry front and back of each hand.
10. Throw used paper towels in the trashcan.

Brenda and Darla walked through each step several times and modeled it for Danielle. They simplified the list by coming up with a picture schedule that showed each step needed to wash and dry hands. The following day, they showed the picture schedule to Danielle and practiced each step together. The hardest part of the task was learning to turn off the water after Danielle had rinsed her hands. Two weeks later, she could wash her hands independently with only minimal assistance from an adult.

Figure 5.3   Children with cognitive challenges learn new skills with picture cues.

CLASSROOM SUGGESTIONS FOR CHILDREN WITH COGNITIVE CHALLENGES

1. Plan activities that are specific and concrete. Use real objects whenever possible and try to teach each new activity in the natural environment where the activity is expected to occur. For example, when teaching a child to wash his hands, you would teach that skill standing at the sink in the bathroom.
2. Observe each child throughout the day and try to discover how that child learns best. Some children learn best with visual clues while others need auditory clues to learn a new skill.
3. Teach the child less, not more. Children with cognitive challenges will need to learn new information in small incremental steps. Break down information into essential components and only teach the child what is necessary.
4. Use modeling and imitation to provide extra opportunities to practice.
5. Use a task-analysis approach for teaching a new skill.
6. Give clear concrete directions.
7. Help everyone who works with the child understand that he may not learn something in the same manner or as quickly as others, however, he can and will learn.

SUMMARY

Children with cognitive delays:

- Have difficulty understanding new concepts;
- Become upset when their routine is changed, so always let them know what is going to happen next;
- Will need new information to be explained more than once, and may require that the same thing be taught repeatedly before understanding it;
- Learn best when they have the opportunity to practice new concepts;
- Need new concepts and activities broken down into smaller steps;
- Become easily frustrated and give up when they think they cannot do something as well or as quickly as others; and
- Have trouble generalizing information across settings and environments.

TERMS USED IN THIS CHAPTER

functional skills—skills that children will use throughout their lives to carry out simple tasks, such as washing, bathing, eating, and dressing; also referred to as life skills or independent living skills.

longitudinal study—a research study that follows the same group of participants across designated points in time.

mental retardation (cognitive delay, intellectual disability)—used to indicate a pattern of learning that is slower than that of typically developing children. This slower pattern of learning may be in areas of development, such as basic motor skills, speech and language skills, self-help skills, or problem-solving skills.

task analysis—the process of designing a step-by-step guide for completing a skill or task.

RESOURCES USED IN THIS CHAPTER

Guralnick, M. J., Neville, B., Hammond, M. A., & Connor, R. T. (2007). The friendships of young children with developmental delays: A longitudinal analysis. *Journal of Applied Developmental Psychology, 28*(1), 64–79.

Hebbeler, K., Spiker, D., Bailey, D., Scarborough, A., Mallik, S., Simeonsson, R., et al. (2007). *Early intervention for infants and toddlers with disabilities and their families: Participants, services, and outcomes.* Final report of the National Early Intervention Longitudinal Study (NEILS). Menlo Park, CA: SRI International.

SUGGESTED READING

Eisenhower, A. S., Baker, B. L., & Blacher, J. (2005). Preschool children with intellectual disability: Syndrome specificity, behaviour problems, and maternal well-being. *Journal of Intellectual Disability Research, 49*(9), 657–671.

Guralnick, M. J., Hammond, M. A., & Connor, R. T. (2003). Subtypes of nonsocial play: Comparisons between young children with and without developmental delays. *American Journal on Mental Retardation, 108*(5), 347–362.

Guralnick, M. J., Hammond, M. A., Connor, R. T., & Neville, B. (2006). Stability, change, and correlates of the peer relationships of young children with mild developmental delays. *Child Development, 77*(2), 312–324.

Guralnick, M. J., Neville, B., Connor, R. T., & Hammond, M. A. (2003). Family factors associated with the peer social competence of young children with mild delays [Electronic version]. *American Journal on Mental Retardation, 108*(4), 272–287.

Iverson, J. M., Longobardi, E., & Caselli, M. C. (2003). Relationship between gestures and words in children with Down's syndrome and typically developing children in the early stages of communicative development. *International Journal of Language & Communication Disorders, 38*(2), 179–197.

THE RESEARCH SAYS . . .

Social Development Across Time

A longitudinal study examined the social relationships between children with mild developmental (cognitive) delays and their friends. The study looked at children in early childhood and early elementary school settings. Results revealed increases in many forms of social interaction with very few changes in how children with cognitive delays interact in play situations. Because of their limited ability to interact socially and their lack of long-term friendships, the study found that children with cognitive challenges do not easily develop long-term friendships. These findings are consistent with the hypothesis that children's limited peer-related social competence impacts all aspects of their development of friendships. The authors concluded that strategies designed to help children with delays establish and maintain consistent friendships with peers should be a priority for early childhood programs.

Guralnick, M. J., Neville, B., Hammond, M. A., & Connor, R. T. (2007). The friendships of young children with developmental delays: A longitudinal analysis. *Journal of Applied Developmental Psychology, 28*(1), 64–79.

Children With Atypical Motor Development

6

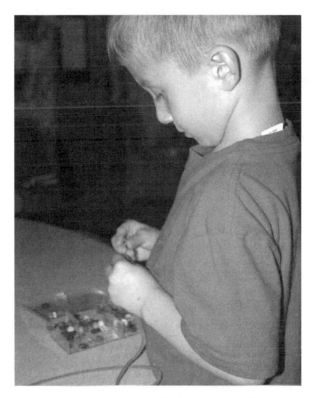

Figure 6.1   Children develop fine motor skills by
stringing beads.

CAUSES OF ATYPICAL MOTOR DEVELOPMENT

Atypical motor development can occur for many reasons including brain
damage occurring before or during birth, orthopedic problems, genetic
defects, developmental delays, and sensory impairments (Hanson & Harris,
1986). Problems in muscle development are usually grouped into one of
the following categories: muscle tone, muscle control, or muscle strength.

MUSCLE TONE

Muscle tone is generally defined as the degree of tension in the muscle when that muscle is at rest. Generally speaking, three types of muscle tone result in a child's having atypical motor development (Martin, 2006):

1. Hypotonic or low muscle tone in which the child appears to be "floppy" or "rag-doll" in her movements. Children who are hypotonic have flaccid muscle tone, especially in their shoulders, hips, and ankles. Because it takes so much effort for the child to move her muscles, she becomes fatigued easily, and usually is less physically active than her peers.

2. Hypertonic is the opposite of hypotonic in that the child's muscles are stiff and rigid. Another term often used interchangeably with hypertonic is spastic. A child who is hypotonic has difficulty with motor movements and his muscles appear to be "locked" in such a way that movement is difficult, especially walking, bending at the knees, or bending the arm at the elbow.

3. A child with a combination of both hypotonic and hypertonic muscle tone is said to have fluctuating muscle tone. This results in difficulty contracting and relaxing muscles. When the child's muscles are relaxed, she appears very floppy or rag-doll like, but when the child starts to move her muscles, they become hypertonic and her movements are very jerky and stiff.

Muscle Control and Strength

A child with difficulty controlling his muscles may exhibit involuntary movements, such as twitches, tremors, or writhing movements, which usually occur because of fluctuating muscle tone. Sometime poor muscle control can result in such characteristics as a child having difficulty opening and closing his mouth or lifting his arms. In extreme cases, a child with very limited muscle control will most likely be confined to a wheelchair and unable to walk or feed himself.

Muscle strength generally refers to what happens when the nervous system communicates a message to the muscle fibers to contract. Often, the force produced by a muscle contraction is against resistance. A child with strong muscles can pick up blocks, play on an outside climbing toy, run fast, and lift objects over her head; a child with poor muscle strength has difficulty with these activities. Some degenerative conditions, such as muscular dystrophy, result in the child losing muscle strength across time. Spinal cord injuries can also result in loss of muscle strength.

CEREBRAL PALSY

The most common motor delay or impairment is cerebral palsy. Cerebral palsy can be caused by many factors and is a broad term used to describe neurological disorders that appear in infancy or early childhood and permanently affect body movement and muscle coordination. In other words, the term is used to describe a variety of conditions that result in the child having permanent difficulty controlling the movement of his muscles. Unlike conditions like muscular dystrophy, cerebral palsy is not degenerative; it will not get worse as the child gets older. Cerebral palsy is caused by malfunctions in the parts of the brain that control muscle movements. Most children with cerebral palsy are born with it, but some have cerebral palsy as the result of brain damage in the first few months or years of life. Brain infections, such as bacterial meningitis or viral encephalitis, or head injury from a motor vehicle accident, a fall, or child abuse can also result in the child being diagnosed with cerebral palsy. Common characteristics include:

- lack of muscle coordination when performing voluntary movements (ataxia),
- stiff or tight muscles and exaggerated or "jerky" movement (spasticity),
- walking with one foot or leg dragging,
- walking on the toes,
- a crouched gait or a "scissored" walk, and
- muscle tone that is either too stiff or too floppy.

FINE AND GROSS MOTOR SKILLS

Helping a child with motor challenges usually involves activities that address either gross motor skills or fine motor skills. Gross motor skills refer to the motor or movement activities where the child uses her entire body, such as walking, running, climbing, and jumping. Gross motor skills include

- balance—ability to maintain equilibrium and stay upright;
- body awareness—posture and control of the head;
- crossing the midline—bringing hands or feet across the center of the body;
- laterality—awareness of the left and right sides of the body;
- major muscle coordination—movement of the muscles;
- spatial orientation—awareness of the body position in space and in relation to other objects or people.

Fine motor skills are those activities involving the fingers, hands, and arms. Eye-hand coordination is also a fine motor skill. Activities that involve fine motor skills development include grasping a pencil, cutting with scissors, stringing beads, and picking up small objects. Table 6.1 outlines some activities that will help a child build fine and gross motor skills.

Table 6.1   Activites for Developing Motor Skills

Fine Motor Skills	*Gross Motor Skills*
Cutting • Cut shapes, curved lines • Cutting different angles • Cut figures with curves and angles • Cutting clay with blunt scissors	Spatial Relations • Ask the child to stand in front of a chair, behind a chair • Practice placing large blocks in, under, beneath, and on top of each other
Pasting • Paste, using a variety of forms (e.g., blocks, felt, paper, string, yarn, cereal, cotton) • Match shapes, color, or pictures to a page and paste them within the outlines	Throwing • Throwing a ball with two hands • Throwing a ball over your head • Pitch a beanbag back and forth with a friend, moving one step back each time
Tracing • Tracing shapes, letters, objects • Tracing numbers • Sitting in a circle and tracing letters with fingers on the back of the child next to him	Laterality • Practicing activities using left hand or right hand • Using terms like turn to the right, turn to the left • Sing the "Hokey-Pokey"
Self-Help Skills • Buttoning, zipping, lacing • Using tools, such as a screwdriver or hammer • Opening/closing a jar • Rolling out Playdoh™ with a rolling pin	Legs/Arms • Galloping like a horse • Jumping a rope • Riding a bike • Walking, while swinging arms back and forth
Prewriting • Scribbling on paper • Connecting the dots • Folding paper into shapes	Moving trunk • Dancing to music • Singing songs that require movements • Moving like animals that creep, crawl, and gallop
Writing • Have the child write in the air with her fingers • To increase his tactile awareness, have the child trace over letters on textured surfaces • When a writing tool is introduced, letters that involve similar strokes should be taught first (moving simple to complex) • Next, teach combinations of letters in short words, sentences, and finally spontaneous writing	Balancing • Invite the child to balance on one foot • Hop on one foot with a friend • Play games like "Red-rover, red-rover" • Walk a pretend tight rope • Walk across an imaginary bridge • Walk with a book on your head

Figure 6.2   Gluing activities help build fine motor skills.

POSITIONING AND HANDLING

While movement is important, there are times when the child will not be moving. During those times, it is imperative that her body be placed into positions that optimize her motor skills and help control atypical reflexes and involuntary movements. The child's physical therapist will help you learn how to position the child for certain daily activities, such as large group time or working in centers. In addition, certain general positioning and handling techniques are useful. Positioning involves placing the child in a position that stabilizes the body and/or normalizes muscle tone. Stabilizing a child's trunk for activities that require sitting should allow her to use her arms with more control.

It should be emphasized that the position of a child should be as natural as possible and similar to the way in which other children in the classroom might be positioned. The child should be situated so he can participate in class activities as much as possible. Keep the child at the same level as other children, as this makes communication and social interaction easier. When an activity is conducted on the floor, position the child on the floor with appropriate support such as an adapted chair or adult body. When carrying the child, try to hold the child in a manner that allows him to visually inspect the environment and socialize with others while helping build strength. Also, consider the child's choice and preferences when implementing positioning and handling strategies. Allow the child to select positions and areas where he would like to play, and remember to give the child the opportunity to perform as much of the movement as possible for himself.

Handling refers to the way a child is lifted. Generally speaking, when lifting a child, keep her head upright and stabilized so that muscle tone can be as normal as possible. When lifting the child, tell her that you are going to lift her and ask her to help in any way possible. Lift the child gently and protect yourself from back injuries by bending your knees and keeping your back straight as you lift.

ADAPTIVE EQUIPMENT

In some cases, a child may require adaptive equipment in order to stand, sit, or walk. The child's physical therapist will help you learn to position the child in his adaptive device or wheelchair. Adaptive equipment for children with motor issues may include the following:

- wheelchair or walker for getting around in the classroom
- specialized chair that enables the child to sit with his back straight
- prone stander, to help the child stand for activities that require standing, such as washing his hands or working at a table.

Remember that other children should be in chairs around the child in the wheelchair, so that all children are at the same eye level. This prevents the child from straining her neck and encourages interactions that are more natural.

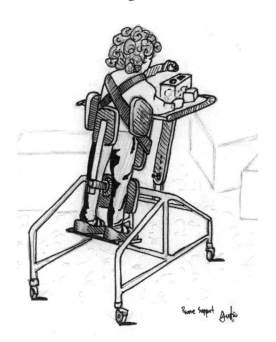

Figure 6.3 Children with motor delays often require mobility aids, such as a prone stander.
Illustration by Justin Mitchel

SUMMARY

Remember, it is very important that the child is seated or positioned so that he can participate as much as possible in daily activities. Even if he cannot do exactly what the other children are doing, he can partially participate in activities. If the child needs adaptive equipment, work closely with the physical therapist to learn how to use the equipment so that it is comfortable for the child, while giving him access to what is going on around him. Also, be sure that aisles and classroom areas are wide enough to accommodate a wheelchair or walker. Be creative and think about ways to help the child with motor delays actively engage in activities with peers, while keeping in mind that he may tire easily because of the extra effort he expends to use his muscles.

TERMS USED IN THIS CHAPTER

ataxia—a lack of muscle coordination when performing voluntary movements.

cerebral palsy—a broad term used to describe neurological disorders that appear in infancy or early childhood and permanently affect body movement and muscle coordination.

degenerative—a medical condition that will get worse as the child gets older.

fluctuating muscle tone—word used to describe muscle tone that is a combination of both hypertonic and hypotonic muscle tone.

hypertonic—the child's muscles are stiff and rigid.

hypotonic—low muscle tone in which the child appears to be "floppy" or "rag-doll" in her movements.

muscular dystrophy—a degenerative condition that results in the child losing muscle strength across time.

spasticity—stiff or tight muscles and exaggerated or "jerky" movement.

RESOURCES USED IN THIS CHAPTER

Hanson, M. J., & Harris, S. R. (1986). *Teaching young children with motor delays: A guide for parents and professionals.* Austin, TX: Pro-Ed.

Harper, L. V., & McCluskey, K. S. (2002). Caregiver and peer responses to children with language and motor disabilities in inclusive preschool programs. *Early Childhood Research Quarterly, 17*(2), 148–166.

Martin, S. (2006). *Teaching motor skills to children with cerebral palsy.* Bethesda, MD: Woodbine House.

SUGGESTED READING

Abbott, A., Bartlett, D. J., Kneale Fanning, J. E., & Kramer, J. (2000). Infant motor development and aspects of the home environment. *Pediatric Physical Therapy, 12*(2), 62–67.

Bruni, M. (2006). *Fine motor skills for children with Down syndrome* (2nd ed). Bethesda, MD: Woodbine House.

Sieglinde, M. (2006). *Teaching motor skills to children with cerebral palsy and similar movement disorders: A guide for parents and professionals.* Bethesda, MD: Woodbine House.

THE RESEARCH SAYS . . .

Children With Motor Delays Are At Risk for Social Isolation

The free-play social behaviors of 24 children with special needs in two discovery-oriented, inclusive preschool programs were compared with their classmates without special needs who were matched by age and sex. Researchers found that children who were incapable of independent locomotion throughout the classroom were largely dependent on adults for initiating changes in their activities and for social exchanges. The researchers found that children with motor delays received more adult support than children developing typically and were at a higher risk of social isolation than children with disabilities who were capable of independent locomotion. Adults' behavior varied according to child condition and activity. From observing a single, 20-minute videotape of free play, naïve observers found the same results in 78 percent of the samples taken. They concluded that had it not been for almost constant adult supervision and facilitation, the children who were incapable of independent locomotion would have been essentially isolated. Therefore, enrolling a child with severe motor handicaps requires adults to look for strategies that will ensure that the child with motor impairments who is unable to move about independently will not be isolated socially or physically from ongoing classroom activities.

Harper, L. V., & McCluskey, K. S. (2002). Caregiver and peer responses to children with language and motor disabilities in inclusive preschool programs. *Early Childhood Research Quarterly, 17*(2), 148–166.

Children With Communication Delays

7

Figure 7.1 Authentic materials help build communication skills.

WHAT IS COMMUNICATION?

Communication is an interaction between two or more people where information is sent between one person and another. The most common method of communicating information is speech. The information that is sent and received is generally referred to as language. Delayed speech and/or language development is the most common developmental problem in preschool children. Although statistics vary, it is believed that speech and/

or language delays affect five to ten percent of four- and five-year-old children. How well a child communicates depends on three aspects of communication: form, function, and content.

Table 7.1   Communication Components

Communication	Definition	Example
Form	A way to communicate	Crying, talking, gesturing, using sign language, pointing to picture cards
Function	A reason to communicate	Feel hungry, want something, need something or someone, need attention
Content	Something to communicate about	The experiences and opportunities to explore that provide the child with something to talk about

UNDERSTANDING THE CHILD'S "FORM" OF COMMUNICATION

For most preschool children, the form of communication they use will be speech. Generally, speech is the sound that is generated when we talk to others. Articulation has to do with how sounds are pronounced. When the sounds within words cannot be understood, it is referred to as misarticulation. In fact, the most common speech delay seen in young children is an articulation delay, such as when a child says "ookee" instead of "cookie." However, it is very important that teachers, families, and caregivers recognize that, as a child is learning to talk, misarticulating is a normal part of the process. For that reason, teachers need to be aware of which sounds are "typical" for a child's age and stage of development. Since all children do not develop at the same pace, there is a range in which specific sounds are thought to develop. When a child's speech is developing more slowly than his peers, the term speech delay or developmental speech delay may be used. However, when these delays persist, as the child matures, the child may be diagnosed with a speech disorder or an articulation disorder.

A few "red flags" that indicate a child may have an articulation problem that is beyond the scope of typical development include

- not talking clearly enough for the teacher to understand much of what is said;
- inconsistent substitution (t/k), such as when the child might say "tookie" instead of the word "cookie," or omission (leaving out) sounds;

- inability to combine common sounds into words; and
- not producing enough speech sounds to combine them into words.

Stuttering is an additional speech problem sometimes noticed in preschool children. While hesitation and repetition of sounds are normal, prolonged repetition and difficulty with airflow when speaking are not. A professional speech-language pathologist can help determine the difference.

FUNCTION AND CONTENT OF COMMUNICATION

The reason a child communicates, as well as what she communicates about, depends on how she uses words to convey her message. Communication generally has two components: receptive language and expressive language. Receptive language involves how well children might respond as they understand what someone is saying to them. Expressive language has to do with how well a child uses or responds with words and sentences. The term language delay is generally used to describe a child whose language is developing in the right sequence, but at a slower rate than her peers. A language disorder describes atypical language development, such as using limited words, no words at all, or not combining words into sentences.

There are generally four components that are considered part of language acquisition. Both reception and production of language use these four basic structural components:

1. Phonology—the system of the sound segments that humans use to build up words. Each language has a different set of these segments or phonemes; children quickly come to recognize and then produce the speech segments that are characteristic of their native language. In fact, current brain research indicates that by the time a child is nine months old, he recognizes sounds that are characteristic of his native language.

2. Semantics—the system of meanings that are expressed by words and phrases. In order to serve as a means of communication between people, words must have a shared or conventional meaning. Conventional meaning may be specific to the subculture or geographic location in which a child lives. For example, the word "pop" may mean soda pop in some geographical areas while the same word "pop" may mean father in other areas. That is why language is often best learned in context, rather than in isolation. Picking out the correct meaning for each new word is a major learning task for many young children. In fact, research has shown a direct correlation between the number of words a child hears by a certain age and her later language acquisition (Singer, Golinkoff, & Hirsh-Pasek, 2006).

Different Meaning of the word

3. Grammar—the system of rules by which words and phrases are arranged to make meaningful statements. Generally speaking, children will learn the names of words (nouns) first, and then they will begin to assign action words (verbs) to their actions. Adjective and descriptive words develop later as the child begins to experiment and use language, not only as a means to get what he needs or wants, but, as a means to describe his world and the people in it.

4. Pragmatics—the system of patterns that determine how humans use language in particular social settings for particular conversational purposes. Children learn that conversation customarily begins with a greeting and requires taking turns. In addition, they learn that conversation usually involves a shared topic. With practice, children learn to adjust the content of their communication to match their listener's interests, knowledge, and language ability. Pragmatics is considered by many the most difficult aspect of language for a child to master.

These "red flags" may be warning signs that a preschool child has a language problem:

- expresses herself with one word;
- has difficulty following simple one- or two-step directions;
- unable to answer a simple question;
- does not initiate conversations with adults or peers;
- does not use verbs, only nouns;
- difficulty describing what she wants or needs; or
- nonverbal (does not talk at all).

THE NONVERBAL CHILD

Some children are nonverbal, meaning that they communicate without using words. An example of a nonverbal child might be one who is selectively mute or just does not talk at all. Just because a child is nonverbal does not mean that he cannot or will not communicate. It simply means we must look for alternative ways to teach him to communicate. One of the most well-known forms of nonverbal communication is sign language. For more information on the use of sign language with children who are hearing impaired, see Chapter 5. Sign language can also be an effective tool for a child without hearing impairments. It can bridge the gap between verbal and nonverbal communication. Often teachers feel that teaching a child basic signs, such as bathroom, eat, drink, outside, etc., will hinder the child's learning to talk. In reality, the opposite is true for many children; it provides a method or form of communication the child can use until he learns to use words.

A few children will never use spoken language as their primary form of communication. For these children, it may be necessary to use an alternative or augmentative form of communication. These augmentative forms of communication generally fall into two categories: low tech and high tech. Low-tech alternative communication tools may include such things as pictures or objects, which the child either points to or selects as a way to tell you what she wants or needs. High-tech communication generally falls into the realm of a battery-operated device that the child activates in some manner and which talks for the child.

Figure 7.2 Children with communication delays can use pictures to communicate.

CLEFT LIP AND PALATE

A cleft palate involves an opening or split in the oral structures that can be surgically repaired at an early age (starting at 12 months). Although the surgeon may be successful in closing the cleft, a fistula (reopening of the palate following surgery) is possible any time after surgery. Whether or not a fistula occurs, it is possible that difficulty with speech may develop. Problems with language delay can also occur due to a child's inability to produce certain sounds.

With cleft palate, it is difficult for children to build up enough oral pressure to produce oral consonants that require a stop of air (*p, b, t, d, k, g, s, sh, ch,* and *f*). Therefore, these sounds may end up being nasalized, meaning the air is sent through the nasal cavity instead of the oral cavity when producing the sounds. For example, "ball" may be pronounced as "mall," because air escapes through the nose and distorts the oral consonant. Even if the child does not have a fistula, the child may have learned compensatory ways to produce these sounds; thus, it is a habit that must be broken.

Articulation can also be affected if the soft palate cannot reach the pharyngeal wall (wall at the back of the throat), causing air to leak through the nose during speech. This is referred to as hypernasal speech and will have a very nasal quality to it, much like how someone sounds with a stuffy nose.

Language delays are prevalent for children who have cleft palate primarily because they have limited speech sounds; additionally, there is a high probability that they will also have a limited vocabulary. Estrem and Broen (1989) and Broen, Devers, Doyle, Prouty, and Moller (1998) studied children with cleft lip and/or palate and children without clefts during acquisition of their first 50 words. These studies found slower vocabulary acquisition for the children with cleft lip and/or palate than for the children without clefts. Further, the studies indicated that children with cleft lip and/or palate chose more words that contained sounds not affected by the structural impairment (nasal sounds and vowels) than the children without clefts, suggesting a possible interaction between sound choice and vocabulary use.

CHILDHOOD APRAXIA OF SPEECH (CAS)

Childhood apraxia of speech (CAS) is a motor speech disorder. Children with CAS have problems saying sounds, syllables, and words. This results not from muscle weakness or paralysis, but from the brain. The brain has difficulty planning movement of the body parts needed for speech. The child knows what he wants to say, but his brain has difficulty coordinating the muscle movements necessary to say those words. The severity of CAS can range from mild to severe. While the causes are still unknown and being researched, some scientists believe it is genetic and others believe it is related to the child's language development process. Generally speaking, a child with CAS will

- make inconsistent sound errors that are not a result of immaturity,
- understand language but seem unable to use it effectively,
- have difficulty imitating speech, and
- have more difficulty saying longer words.

A child can be evaluated for the speech problems by a certified speech-language pathologist (SLP) who will assess the child's oral motor abilities, melody of speech, and speech sound development. The SLP can further rule out any other speech disorder. If the child has CAS, the SLP will most likely recommend individual treatment two to five times a week, depending on the severity. Since every child is different, it is recommended that teachers speak with the child's SLP to obtain some tips on how to decrease the child's communication pressure in the classroom.

TERMS USED IN THIS CHAPTER

articulation disorder   a type of speech delay where one sound is either substituted for another sound, omitted, or distorted in such a way that it is not clearly understood.

childhood apraxia of speech (CAS)—a speech problem that occurs when the brain tries to tell the muscles what to do—somehow, that message gets scrambled and the child's ability to speak is affected.

fistula—a condition that occurs when a cleft palate has been surgically repaired but fails to heal properly or the primary surgical repair breaks down.

language delay—used to describe the overall language functioning of a child who is below that of typically developing children.

language disorder—a significant language delay that is usually not attributed to delayed development or lack of opportunity to use language.

misarticulation—a speech problem resulting in the child mispronouncing a sound or omitting it all together.

speech delay—when the child's speech is delayed due to immaturity or a physiological reason.

RESOURCES USED IN THIS CHAPTER

Barber, M. (2007). Imitation, interaction and dialogue using Intensive Interaction: Tea party rules. *Support for Learning, 22*(3), 124–130.

Broen, P. A., Devers, M., Doyle, S. S., Prouty, J. M., & Moller, K. T. (1998). Acquisition of linguistic and cognitive skills by children with cleft palate. *Journal of Speech and Hearing Research, 41*(3), 76–87.

Estrem, T., & Broen, P. A. (1989). Early speech production of children with cleft palate. *Journal of Speech and Hearing Research, 32*(1), 12–23.

Singer, D., Golinkoff, R. M., Hirsh-Pasek, K. (Eds.). (2006). *Play = Learning: How play motivates and enhances children's cognitive and social emotional growth.* Oxford, NY: Oxford University Press.

SUGGESTED READING

Bird, J., Bishop, D. V. M., & Freeman, N. (1995). Phonological awareness and literacy development in children with expressive phonological impairments. *Journal of Speech and Hearing Research, 38*(4), 446–462.

Dahlgren Sandberg, A. (2001). Reading and spelling, phonological awareness, and working memory in children with severe speech impairments: A longitudinal study. *Augmentative and Alternative Communication, 17*(1), 11–26.

Kaderavek, J., & Rabidoux, P. (2004). Interactive to independent literacy: A model for designing literacy goals for children with atypical communication. *Reading and Writing Quarterly, 20*(3), 237–260.

Koppenhaver, D., & Erickson, K. (2003). Natural emergent literacy supports for preschoolers with autism and severe communication impairments. *Topics in Language Disorders, 23*(4), 283–292.

Kumin, L. (2003). *Early communication skills for children with Down syndrome.* Bethesda, MD: Woodbine House.

Schwartz, S. (2004). *The new language of toys: Teaching communication skills to children with special needs—a guide for parents and teachers,* (2nd ed.). Bethesda, MD: Woodbine House.

Sturm, J., & Clendon, S. (2004). Augmentative and alternative communication, language, and literacy: Fostering the relationship. *Topics in Language Disorders, 24*(1), 76–91.

THE RESEARCH SAYS . . .

Communication Is More Than Just Imitation

Intensive interactions have become a widely used method for helping children with special needs increase their communication skills. Most of these strategies have involved teachers using imitation as a primary response method. In a recent research article, Mark Barber (2007) discusses how imitation limits those kinds of interactions that children with special needs have with peers. The article explores how, instead of just imitating, practitioners need to develop other guidelines that help children learn to communicate in a reciprocal manner. These might include such things as following the child's lead, introducing closely related ideas in a way that is meaningful to children, and providing variations in how children communicate with each other. He refers to these positive interactions as the "tea-party rules" developed by typically developing young children at play.

Barber, M. (2007). Imitation, interaction and dialogue using Intensive Interaction: Tea party rules. *Support for Learning, 22*(3), 124–130.

Children With Emotional/ Behavior Disorders

Figure 8.1   Children with challenging behaviors
respond well to one-on-one interaction.

WHAT ARE CHALLENGING BEHAVIORS?

According to Doss and Reichle (1991), "Challenging behaviors (or problem behaviors) result in self-injury, injury to others, cause damage to the physical environment, interfere with the acquisition of new skills, and/or socially isolate the learner." In other words, challenging behaviors are actions by the child that cause an interruption of her learning or the learning of those around her. The types of challenging behavior that you may find in an early childhood classroom could be the result of, but are not limited to, any one of the following: a general anxiety disorder, the effect of some event that involved the child resulting in post-traumatic stress disorder (PTSD), or a conduct disorder.

YOUNG CHILDREN AND MENTAL HEALTH

Defining mental health in children is difficult; because compared to other mental health issues, it is a relatively new field. In general, a child is considered to be at risk for mental illness when

- the symptoms occur often and last a long time (several months),
- the symptoms are present in more than one setting (school, home, community), and
- the symptoms cause distress and impair normal functioning (Bilmes & Welker, 2006).

Several factors can influence a child's mental health, including the overall temperament and genetic predisposition of the child, the child's relationship with his family, and the child's environment.

ANXIETY DISORDERS

While it is now estimated that more than 12 percent of preteens and teenagers have an anxiety disorder, it has only been during the last few years that anxiety disorders have been recognized in children at all. In general, a child is considered to have an anxiety disorder in the following circumstances:

- When fear-related or avoidance behavior prevents the child from doing the things that she would otherwise want to do.
- When a child displays a behavior beyond the age when she is expected to do so. For instance, separation anxiety in a two-year-old could well be transient and is considered quite normal; in an older child, it is a disorder.
- Children normally go through phases of obsessive behavior, but, when it continues to the point of interrupting daily activities, it becomes a disorder.

In summary, the main characteristics of a general anxiety disorder include worrying about things or events that are not real, somatic (physical) ailments that are not related to an actual illness, tension that is prolonged, and difficulty relaxing (Chansky, 2006).

CLASSROOM SUGGESTIONS FOR CHILDREN WITH ANXIETY DISORDERS

The following are suggestions that enable the teacher to help the child with general anxiety-disorder function in the early childhood classroom:

1. Try to help the child learn problem-solving techniques.
2. Develop routines that foster independence.
3. Keep the child engaged and involved in activities.
4. Respect his issues, but don't "play into" them by allowing the child to constantly discuss them.
5. Be consistent, yet patient, with the child and remember his anxiety is very real.

SEPARATION ANXIETY

While there are many kinds of anxiety disorders, separation anxiety is one of the most common anxiety disorders found in children. Fear of separation from a parent is very common in young children and, in some ways, is part of a child's normal development. However, by the time the child is in preschool, this fear should only be manifested occasionally—for example, during the first week of a new school year. Characteristics of separation anxiety include:

- persistent unrealistic fear that some destructive event will happen that prevents return of the adult or that the adult will not return at all;
- apprehension that something will happen to increase the child's separation from the adult;
- unwillingness to sleep without the adult;
- avoidance of other children after being left by the adult;
- physical manifestations—stomachache, headache, vomiting, etc.;
- repeated signs of distress—tantrums, crying, or pleading not to leave;
- repeated need to speak with the adult, call the adult at work, or be near the adult at all times (Foxman, 2006).

CLASSROOM SUGGESTIONS FOR CHILDREN WITH SEPARATION ANXIETY

The following guidelines can help the teacher reassure a child with separation anxiety:

[handwritten: separation with parents]

1. Help the child feel safe and reassured that the adult will return, but don't allow her to dwell on it.
2. Help the child develop social skills to cope with being left. As the child feels more confident, she may be less anxious.
3. Encourage routines that help the child feel secure.
4. Make sure the child has time to transition and calm down after getting upset. *[handwritten: activities]*
5. Work with the child to help her recognize that her parent will return.

POST-TRAUMATIC STRESS DISORDER (PTSD)

Post-traumatic stress disorder (PTSD) is diagnosed when a child has witnessed a catastrophic event that has traumatized him, thus resulting in his being unable to function as he normally would. In order to be diagnosed with PTSD, a child must have been exposed to a traumatic event and must have experienced symptoms for more than one month (Crist, 2004).

Table 8.1   Major Symptoms of Post-Traumatic Stress Disorder (PTSD)

1. Child expresses at least one of the following:
   - Uses play to reenact the trauma;
   - Continues to discuss the event;
   - Frequent terrors at night, including vivid nightmares;
   - Becomes physically ill when triggered about event; or
   - Experiences flashbacks and periods of "spacing out."

2. Child withdraws from the world and pulls into herself:
   - Interacts less frequently with others,
   - Shows grossly inappropriate emotions or no emotion at all,
   - Shows decreased interest in daily routines, or
   - Avoids people and events that remind her of the trauma.

3. Child seems tense and "edgy" in at least two areas:
   - Sleep—either sleeps too long, too little, or does not stay asleep;
   - Distracted by insignificant things;
   - Hypervigilance—overly aware of small environmental changes;
   - Outbursts of tantrums or anger; or
   - Startles easily at happy things.

4. Other possible symptoms (not always present):
- Loss of previously acquired skills,
- Becoming aggressive or violent, or
- Afraid of things that did not scare her in the past or things that are not normally feared by children.

CLASSROOM SUGGESTIONS FOR CHILDREN WITH PTSD

Teachers must remember that a child with PTSD will need extra patience and attention. In addition, certain activities and/or events can trigger the memory of the event; the result may be that the child gets very upset over something that, to the teacher and his classmates, is insignificant or meaningless. These suggestions can help the teacher who has a child with PTSD in the classroom:

1. Help the child feel safe and try to use a soft voice whenever possible.
2. Help the child manage and identify his emotions.
3. Work with the child's family and therapist to learn what they feel is appropriate for you to discuss with the child about the event.
4. When possible, help the child understand what has happened.
5. Answer questions as frankly and as often as they are asked. The worst possible thing that can be done with a child with PTSD is to ignore it and treat the event like it never happened.
6. Learn to recognize what activities or events trigger the event and, later, try to teach the child to recognize those triggers as well.

OPPOSITIONAL DEFIANT DISORDER (ODD)

When behavior becomes very challenging and disruptive on a daily basis, and nothing the teacher does seems to alleviate it, the child could have a disorder known as oppositional defiant disorder (ODD). The *Diagnostic and Statistical Manual of Mental Disorders* (DSM-IV) of the American Psychiatric Association (2000) defines ODD as a condition in which the child shows "a pattern of negativistic, hostile, and defiant behavior lasting at least six months," for which at least four of the following behaviors are present:

1. The child often loses her temper to the extreme;
2. The child argues with adults about everything;

3. The child often actively defies or refuses to cooperate with adult requests or rules;
4. The child deliberately annoys people;
5. The child blames others constantly for her mistakes or misbehavior;
6. The child is touchy or easily annoyed by others or gets mad over insignificant events;
7. The child seems angry and resentful most of the time; or
8. The child is very spiteful, vindictive, or wants to punish others for what she believes to be injustices toward her.

To be diagnosed with ODD, the child must exhibit the behaviors much more often than would be expected for children at this age and stage of development. In addition, his challenging behaviors must interfere with his learning and social interactions with others. The best source of information about the child will come from his family. Often, families of children with ODD describe violent and uncontrollable temper tantrums and frequent battles over everyday tasks, like eating breakfast or going to bed at night. Parents may report that their child has been removed from other preschool programs because of his behavior or that no one, not even family members, will babysit for the child. In some cases, a child may develop a more serious behavior problem, known as conduct disorder. Conduct disorder includes problems of violence toward people or animals, destruction of property, theft or shoplifting, and serious problems following rules at school or at home.

ODD can be treated if diagnosed early and if intervention begins in preschool or early school years. While a child with ODD will not necessarily develop full-blown conduct disorder, the likelihood is greater if the behaviors are ignored until the child is older.

CLASSROOM SUGGESTIONS FOR CHILDREN WITH ODD

1. Keep routines simple.
2. Make sure the rules are clear, specific, and consistently enforced.
3. Deal with behaviors as they occur and work closely with the child's family and therapist to monitor her progress. Make sure you and the child's family have a specific and consistent method to communicate with each other.
4. Try to keep the child actively engaged in daily activities as much as possible.

ATTENTION-DEFICIT/HYPERACTIVITY DISORDER (ADHD)

According to the American Psychiatric Association (2000), the term attention-deficit/hyperactivity disorder (ADHD) is used to describe a neurobehavioral condition that is often characterized by excessive restlessness, inattention, distraction, and impulsivity. While it is usually first noticed when children are entering school, it can be diagnosed in people of all ages. According to the National Institute of Mental Health, in an average classroom of 30 children, research suggests that at least one will have ADHD (NIMH, 2000).

No single cause for ADHD has been identified. However, recent research indicates that genes inherited from parents could be the primary contributor to a child having ADHD. Studies clearly show that ADHD runs in families—76 percent of children with ADHD have a relative with the condition Faraone & Biederman (2000). In order to be diagnosed with ADHD, a child must have symptoms that impair his ability to function as well as other children the same age, and these symptoms must last at least six months (American Psychiatric Association, 2000)

Some of the most common characteristics of ADHD include:

- Inability to pay attention—While we know that young children have very short attention spans, this behavior goes beyond the norm in its intensity. A young child might have difficulty staying focused and attending to a task. She may be easily distracted by irrelevant sights and sounds and shift from one activity to another without finishing a task. Organizing and completing tasks are often extremely difficult because the child with ADHD is so busy moving to the next task that she forgets to finish the one she just started.

- Hyperactivity—Children who have hyperactivity appear to be in constant motion. In other words, they are continually "on the go." The child might have difficulty sitting still and may squirm or fidget. In addition, children with hyperactivity often feel restless, may talk excessively, and display disruptive behaviors.

- Impulsive—Children who are impulsive will "act before thinking." They may interrupt others, blurt out responses, and have difficulty waiting their turn. Other symptoms may manifest as a child who is constantly interrupting the teacher or who gets very angry when he has to wait.

There are three subtypes of ADHD: primarily inattentive, where the symptoms are related to inattention and not to impulsivity; primarily hyperactive/impulsive, in which the symptoms are more in line with being hyperactive and unable to control impulses; and those with combined symptoms of all three (hyperactive, inattentive, and impulse control).

MEDICATION ISSUES

In many cases, treatment for ADHD involves both a behavior treatment plan and medication. The National Institute of Mental Health (NIMH) conducted the most in-depth study to date for evaluating ADHD treatments. The study is called the Multi-modal Treatment Study of Children with ADHD (or the MTA). Data from this study showed that methylphenidate (a commonly used stimulant medication for ADHD) is effective in treating the symptoms of ADHD, either alone or in combination with behavioral therapy (National Institute of Mental Health, 2000). "An additional study funded by the NIMH which looked specifically at preschoolers with ADHD found that those without other co-existing disorders had the most success with medication to control the behaviors associated with ADHD" (Ghuman et al., 2007). The choice to use medication is a medical decision and for the purposes of this book, only the aspects of a behavior plan will be discussed.

Behavioral treatments in the MTA study included three approaches:

- Parent training—Help parents learn about ADHD and ways to manage ADHD behaviors.
- Child-focused treatment—Help children learn to develop social, academic, and problem-solving skills.
- School-based intervention—Help teachers meet children's educational needs by teaching them skills to manage the children's ADHD behaviors in the classroom (such as rewards, consequences, and daily report cards sent to parents).

CLASSROOM SUGGESTIONS FOR CHILDREN WITH ADHD

Children with ADHD usually have significant difficulty forming friendships and learning social skills. In addition, they need extra support organizing materials and staying on task. These are some suggestions that may help:

1. Keep rules simple and enforce them consistently.
2. Provide guides, such as picture cards to help the child remember classroom rules.
3. Practice specific social skills, such as waiting for a turn or asking for a toy.

4. Help the child learn to organize his materials; for example, use a folder in a specific color such as red for finished work or for information to be sent home.

5. Keep in constant communication with the child's family. If possible, use a daily notebook to jot down information directed to the family and for them to provide you with information. Something as simple as knowing the child stayed up late the night before can significantly impact how you plan the day's instruction for the child.

Figure 8.2   Music and dance help reinforce positive behavior.

6. If the child is on medication, make sure you know when he is to receive it and how it will be administered.

7. Praise the child when he completes a task or activity.

8. Provide an avenue for the child to let you know when he needs to get up and move around. This could be as simple as having a "movement" center where the child can go to dance to music when he needs to move.

9. Work with the child's family to develop a systematic method for rewarding positive behavior.

10. If services are available, playgroups or support groups for children with ADHD can be very effective.

SUMMARY

Whether the child has ADHD, mental health issues, or has diagnosed behavioral issues, there are a few general suggestions that may enable a teacher to help the child deal with issues surrounding her challenging behaviors:

1. Work on relaxation techniques with the child, such as counting to five or taking a deep breath.
2. Make a list of things with the child that are relaxing for her.
3. When appropriate, encourage the child to draw what she worries about or talk about it with an adult.
4. Make a brightly colored box for the classroom and encourage children to place their worries in the box.

Figure 8.3   Children with anxiety disorders may benefit from art therapy. *Illustration by Justin Mitchel*

5. Do not let the child dwell on her worries or concerns after she talks about them. Take the approach that now it is time to work.
6. Use music as a way to relax.
7. Keep rules simple; be consistent with enforcement of the rules.
8. Consider ways to help her relieve stress, such as yoga or exercise.
9. Communicate frequently with the child's family about her progress.

TERMS USED IN THIS CHAPTER

anxiety disorder—when a child worries about things or events that are not real, consistently has somatic (physical) ailments that are not related to an actual illness, displays tension that is prolonged, and/or is so overwrought that it consistently interferes with daily life.

attention-deficit/hyperactivity disorder (ADHD)—a neurobehavioral condition, which is often characterized by excessive restlessness, inattention, distraction, and impulsivity.

challenging behavior—actions by the child that result in an interruption of her learning or the learning of those around her and may include such things as self-injury, aggression toward others, and violent outbursts.

conduct disorder—includes problems of violence toward people or animals, destruction of property, theft or shoplifting, and serious problems following rules at school or at home.

methylphenidate—a medication that is a commonly used stimulant for attention-deficit/hyperactivity disorder (ADHD).

oppositional defiant disorder (ODD)—used to describe a child with a pattern of negativistic, hostile, and defiant behavior that is extreme in nature and occurs for at least six months.

post-traumatic stress disorder (PTSD)—a condition, diagnosed when a child has witnessed a catastrophic event that has traumatized him, thus resulting in his being unable to function as he normally would.

RESOURCES USED IN THIS CHAPTER

American Psychiatric Association. (2000). *Diagnostic and statistical manual of mental disorders* (4th ed.). Washington, DC: American Psychiatric Press, Inc.

Bilmes, J., & Welker, T. (2006). *Common psychological disorders in children: A handbook for child care professionals.* St. Paul, MN: Redleaf Press.

Chansky, T. (2006). *Freeing your child from anxiety.* New York: Broadway Books.

Crist, J. J. (2004). *What to do when you're scared and worried: A guide for kids.* Minneapolis, MN: Free Spirit Publishing.

Doss, L. S., & Riechle, J. (1991). Replacing excess behavior with an initial communicative repertoire. In J. Reichle, J. York, & J. Sigafoos (Eds.), *Implementing augmentative and alternative communication: Strategies for learners with severe disabilities.* Baltimore, MD: Brooks Publishing Co.

Faraone, S. V., & Beiderman, J. (2000). Nature, nurture, and attention deficit hyperactivity disorder. *Developmental Review, 20*(4), 568–581.

Foxman, P. (2006). *The worried child: Recognizing anxiety in children and helping them heal.* Alameda, CA: Hunter House Publishing.

Ghuman, J. K., Riddle, M. A., Vitiello, B., Greenhill, L. L., Chuang, S. Z., Wigal, S. B., Kollins, S. H., Abikoff, H. B., McCracken, J. T., Kastelic, E., Scharko, A. M., McGough, J. J., Murray, D. W., Evans, L., Swanson, J. M., Wigal, T., Posner, K., Cunningham, C., Davies, M., & Skrobala, A. M. (2007). Comorbidity moderates response to methylphenidate in the preschoolers with attention-deficit/hyperactivity disorder treatment study (PATS). *Journal of Child and Adolescent Psychopharmacology, 17*(5), 563–580.

National Institute of Mental Health. (2000, March). *Research on treatment for attention deficit hyperactivity disorder (ADHD): Questions and answers about the multimodal treatment study.* Retrieved from http://www.nimh.nih.gov/health/trials/nimh-research-on-treatment-for-attention-deficit-hyperactivity-disorder-adhd-questions-and-answers-about-the-multimodal-treatmen.shtml

Nelson, J. R., Stage, S., Duppong-Hurley, K., Synhorst, L., & Epstein, M. H. (2007). Risk factors predictive of the problem behavior of children at risk for emotional and behavioral disorders. *Exceptional Children, 73*(3), 367–380.

SUGGESTED READING

Buron, Karl Dunn. (2006). *When My Worries Get Too Big! A Relaxation Book for Children Who Live with Anxiety.* Shawnee Mission, KS: Autism Asperger Publishing Company.

Fox, L., Dunlap, G., Hemmeter, M. L., Joseph, G. E., & Strain, P. S. (2003). The teaching pyramid: A model for supporting social competence and preventing challenging behavior in young children. *Young Children, 58*(4), 48–52.

Huebner, Dawn. (2004). *What to Do When You Worry Too Much! A Kid's Guide to Overcoming Anxiety.* Washington, DC: Magination Press-American Psychological Association.

Manassis, Katharina. (1996). *Keys to Parenting Your Anxious Child.* Hauppauge, NY: Barron's Educational Series.

Rosenfield, A., Wise, N., & Coles, R. (2001). *The Overscheduled Child: Avoiding the Hyper-Parenting Trap.* New York: Griffin Publishers.

THE RESEARCH SAYS . . .

Risk Factors for Future Challenging Behaviors

A recent research study used logistic regression analyses to attempt to establish a set of risk factors that would best predict borderline/clinical levels of problem behavior (i.e., a t score at or above 60 on the Child Behavior Checklist Total Problem scale) of kindergarten and first-grade children at risk for emotional and behavioral disorders. The study looked at 11 risk factors in an effort to determine if a relationship existed between those risk factors and future challenging behavior patterns. Results showed 5 of the 11 factors were most predictive of borderline/clinical levels of problem behavior. These five included (a) externalizing patterns of behavior, (b) internalizing behavior patterns, (c) early childhood child maladjustment, (d) family functioning, and (e) maternal depression. Within these five domains, the most risk factors included such things as child temperament, parent management skills, interaction between temperament and parent management skills, destruction of his or her own toys, and maternal depression.

The authors feel this study was successful in identifying certain risk factors that are reasonably accurate predictors of parent/caregiver-reported social behavior of young children. Indeed, in the present study, among a standard list of 40 potential risk factors, three factors (i.e., destroys own toys, difficult child, maternal depression) were found to be the most accurate predictors of problem behavior. This suggests that school personnel and developers of early screening tools for children at risk for behavior disorders consider including items that address these variables. In addition, there was an identified need for comprehensive screening programs to identify young children at risk for such disorders. The authors feel strongly that such programs should include items for parents and caregivers to report on the child's play with toys, early negative parent-child interactions, and maternal depression. The results of the present study suggest that these items will be highly predictive of significant child problem behavior.

Nelson, J. R., Stage, S., Duppong-Hurley, K., Synhorst, L. & Epstein, M. H. (2007).Risk factors predictive of the problem behavior of children at risk for emotional and behavioral disorders. *Exceptional Children, 73*(3), 367–380.

Children With Autism Spectrum Disorder (ASD)

9

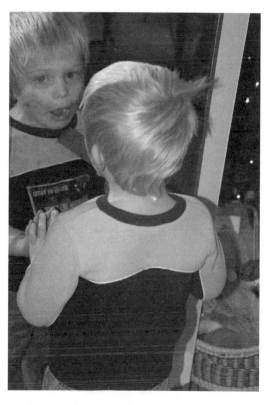

Figure 9.1   Children with autism spectrum disorder may respond differently to their environment.

WHAT IS A SPECTRUM DISORDER?

Children with autism spectrum disorder (ASD) can be especially challenging for early childhood educators, because these children may have one or more of the major characteristics of autism, ranging from very mild to quite severe. In other words, this disorder manifests in many different ways. For that reason, it is referred to as a spectrum disorder, because it includes children with characteristics that range from the mild end to the severe end of the spectrum and everywhere in between.

WHAT IS AUTISM?

Autism is a complex biological disorder that generally lasts throughout a person's life. It starts before age three, during the developmental period, and causes delays or problems in many different areas, including behavior, communication, and social skills acquisition (see Table 9.1). Autism occurs in boys four times more often than it does in girls. Figures released by the Centers for Disease Control indicate that 1 in 150 children will be diagnosed with autism (Autism Information Center, Centers for Disease Control, 2007).

The most accepted definition of autism comes from the *Diagnostic and Statistical Manual of Mental Disorders, Fourth Edition-Text Revision* (DSM-IV-TR) (2000), a manual used by the American Psychiatric Association, as well as most mental health professionals, to diagnose and identify the characteristics of specific psychiatric and emotional disorders. Autism itself falls under the broad category called pervasive development delays (PDD). According to the DSM-IV-TR, to be diagnosed with one of the five types of autism, a child must exhibit delayed or atypical behaviors in at least one of three categories:

1. Interaction with others (social interaction)
2. Communication (response to others)
3. Behavior (examples include bizarre or stereotypical behaviors, such as hand flapping or rocking back and forth)

WHAT ARE THE FIVE TYPES OF AUTISM?

There are five types or categories of autism. While they have similarities, each category is, in some manner, unique, when compared to the others. One way to think about it is to consider ASD as an umbrella shared by several people. Each person is different, while they all share the same umbrella; the same is true of the various types of autism. The recognized types of ASD include

- Autism
- Pervasive developmental disorder not otherwise specified (PDDNOS)
- Asperger syndrome

- Rett's syndrome
- Childhood disintegrative disorder (Heller's syndrome)

Autism: To be diagnosed with autism, a significant number of the following characteristics must clearly be present: a delay in social interaction, such as eye contact or facial expression; a communication delay, such as being nonverbal or using fewer words than peers; behaviors, including stereotypical behavior, such as intense, almost obsessive, preoccupation with objects; the need for routines that are nonfunctional and ritualistic, such as lining up all the books or food in a certain manner; and repeating motor movements again and again, such as rocking back and forth or hand flapping.

Pervasive developmental disorder not otherwise specified (PDD-NOS): This classification, though different, is sometimes confused with PDD, which is the broad category within the DSM-IV-TR in which autism is found. PDD-NOS is used when it is determined that a child has autism, while the characteristics displayed by the child are not like the characteristics of other children with autism. This diagnosis is also used when the onset of the disorder happens after age three. According to the Yale University Developmental Disabilities Clinic (2007), "PDD-NOS is included in DSM-IV to encompass cases where there is marked impairment of social interaction, communication, and/or stereotyped behavior patterns or interest, but when full features for autism or another explicitly defined PDD are not met." Of all the classifications used for autism, this is the most confusing for both families and teachers. However, this classification allows a child with a few, but not all, of the characteristics of autism to be classified as having autism, so that he can receive the needed services.

Asperger syndrome: Children with Asperger syndrome typically behave much like children with other types of autism when they are young, in that they will have some difficulty with communication, social interaction, and/or behaviors. However, as they grow into middle-school-age children or adolescents, they often learn how to socialize, communicate, and behave in a more socially acceptable manner. Most children with Asperger have normal or above normal intelligence, so they learn new skills as fast or, in many cases, faster than their peers without autism. These children have been described as having difficulty with coordination, vocal tone (they tend to speak in a monotone), depression, violent reactions to change, and a tendency for ritualistic behaviors. In addition, children with Asperger syndrome may develop intense obsessions with objects or activities. Unlike other children with ASD, these children tend to develop normally in the areas of self-help and adaptive behaviors, with the only exception appearing in the area of social skills, which is often delayed. Many children with Asperger syndrome can and do function very successfully in blended or inclusive classrooms.

Rett's syndrome: This disorder is also referred to as Rett's disorder and, unlike most of the other types of autism, it worsens with time. For that reason, it is considered a degenerative condition. It begins sometime in the first two years of life and is found almost exclusively in girls. Children with Rett's syndrome develop normally prior to the onset of the disorder. Characteristics include loss of motor skills, hand wringing or repetitive hand movements, and a decrease in head growth. Seizures and sleeping disorders also develop in many girls with this disorder.

Childhood disintegrative disorder: This disorder is sometimes called Heller's syndrome and is also a degenerative condition in which a child may begin to develop normally, but, over a few months, will start to lose or seem to forget how to do things. It usually happens in the areas of toilet training, play skills, language skills, or problem-solving skills. This degeneration or loss of skills usually happens between ages three and four.

As you plan for a child with autism to come into your class, these resources will be helpful to you:

- Up-to-date, accurate information about the primary characteristics of autism, as well as very specific information about the child. This information can be obtained from resources such as the Autism Society of America (ASA), The Autism Information Center at the Centers for Disease Control, Autism Speaks, and the National Autism Association.
- A strong support system that includes specialists, such as early interventionists, special education teachers, speech pathologists, and occupational therapists.
- A positive relationship with the child's family, so that, together, you can share the child's challenges as well as her victories.
- Specific training in how to help with the child's behavior, communication, social skills, self-help skills, and stereotypical behaviors.
- Information about how to create a classroom environment that meets the unique sensory needs of a child with autism (see Chapter 10, "Sensory Integration").

Table 9.1   Major Symptoms of ASD

Social Interaction
<ul><li>Social interaction with other people, both physical (such as hugging or holding) and verbal (such as having a conversation), is impaired.</li><li>Children with ASDs do not interact with other people the way most children do or they may not be interested in other people at all.</li><li>Children with ASDs may not make eye contact and may just want to be alone.</li><li>Children with ASDs may have trouble understanding other people's feelings or talking about their own feelings.</li><li>A child with an ASD may not like to be held or cuddled and may not attach to or bond with other people.</li></ul>
Communication
<ul><li>Communication, both verbal (spoken) and nonverbal (unspoken), will be affected.</li><li>About 40% of children with ASDs do not talk at all. Other children have echolalia, a condition in which they repeat back something that was said to them.</li><li>Children may repeat a television advertisement heard sometime in the past.</li><li>Children with ASDs may not understand gestures, such as waving goodbye. They may say "I" when they mean "you" or vice versa.</li><li>Their voices may sound flat and it may seem like they cannot control how loudly or softly they talk.</li><li>Children with ASDs may stand too close to the people they are talking to or may continue with one topic of conversation for too long.</li></ul>
Behaviors
<ul><li>Children may have routines or repetitive behaviors, like repeating words or actions continually, obsessively following routines or schedules for their actions, or having very specific ways of arranging their belongings.</li><li>Children may want routines where things stay the same, so they know what to expect.</li><li>Children may exhibit stereotypical behaviors, such as hand flapping, hand wringing, rocking, or twisting hair.</li></ul>

BEGIN BY LOOKING AT THE CHILD'S BEHAVIOR

It is important to note that professionals generally agree that most children with autism need help on varying levels with behavior, social skills, and communication. Behavior interventions may include programs designed to help the child decrease ritualistic and stereotypic behaviors and increase acceptable behaviors. Children with autism often develop stereotypic patterns of behavior. Stereotypic or self-stimulatory behavior refers to repetitive body movements or repetitive movement of objects as a form of stimulation. While this behavior is commonly seen in many children with developmental disabilities, it appears to be more common in children with autism. Stereotypic behavior can involve any one or all senses. Some of the most common stereotypic behaviors seen in children with autism are listed in Table 9.2

Table 9.2   Stereotypic Behaviors Commonly Seen in Children With ASD

Sense	*Stereotypic Behaviors*
Visual	Staring at lights, repetitive blinking, moving fingers in front of the eyes, hand flapping, and watching objects such as a fan go around and around
Auditory	Tapping ears, snapping fingers, making vocal sounds, banging on a table, ringing a bell repeatedly, and pounding on piano keys
Tactile	Rubbing the skin with another object or his hands, scratching herself, rubbing self on a scratchy surface like a carpet
Vestibular	Rocking front to back, rocking side to side, and walking on the tips of the toes
Taste	Placing body parts or objects in one's mouth and licking objects
Smell	Smelling objects and sniffing people

Typically developing children learn without our intervention—that is, they learn from an environment that presents conditions conducive for them to learn language, play, and develop social skills. As they get older, they begin to learn more content-specific information, such as reading, writing, and math, in the context of a more structured systematically planned environment.

For example, a child without autism may enter an early childhood setting and watch how other children act, and then model that behavior in his own actions. Children with autism are much less fortunate in that they traditionally do not learn by watching others and picking up environmental cues. This does not mean they are incapable of learning, it simply means that, in order to learn, their instruction must be more explicit. They will benefit from a very structured environment, one where conditions are optimized for acquiring the same skills that typical children learn "naturally." One method that has been used successfully to help children with autism develop more acceptable patterns of behavior is called applied behavior analysis or ABA. This method helps teachers and children establish rules for setting up the environment to enable children with autism learn.

In order for a behavior intervention to be successful, it is important that a functional behavior analysis be conducted. Behavior specialists help teachers and other care providers identify the functions or reasons behind certain behaviors. They also try to identify setting events, such as a change in staff, change in medication, or change in the child's daily routine, that may contribute to the child's behavior. Often, the next step involves the support team (teacher, special educator, behavior specialist, etc.) determining if there is a strategy or method they might use to help the child replace the old behavior (hand flapping, screaming out loud, etc.) with a new, more acceptable, behavior. This is called a communicative replacement.

Let's look at an example of how this could work. Cara is a four-year-old with Asperger syndrome. Every day, she screams if she does not get a dessert immediately following her meal. The screaming soon becomes a full-blown tantrum, which forces the teacher to stop serving lunch to the rest of the class and deal with Cara. After talking with Cara's family, the teacher discovers that the same thing happens at home. Working with the behavior specialist, Cara's teacher and her family determine that they will try to stop the behavior from occurring by developing a behavior plan for Cara. Initially, as Cara begins to finish eating, her teacher and her family take her hand and place it on a picture card featuring a dessert. She is given her dessert immediately. This physical prompt serves as a way to let Cara know what is going to happen next (i.e., she will get a dessert) and help Cara connect the picture card to receiving the actual dessert. Later, they will work with Cara to see if she can tolerate a few seconds delay between the time when she places her hand on the card representing dessert and the time when she actually receives the dessert. The ultimate goal is for Cara to initiate getting her dessert by placing her hand on the card representing dessert and waiting until the dessert is given to her. This goal will take time to develop. The likelihood of success depends on many factors, including the consistency in which the method is used as well as Cara's overall demeanor at each meal.

Another type of behavior that is often seen in children with autism is their ability to "tune out" what is going on around them. A technique known as "hands at home" can sometimes help direct their attention toward the teacher. The teacher holds her hands up in the air (a sign or cue to the class) to indicate to the children they are to put their hands at home. Home could be a designated spot on the table in front of them or by their side. In some cases, the teacher might draw and cut out an outline of the child's hands and affix them to the table, so that, when she gives the signal, the child places his hands on the cut-outs. The next step is for the children to look at the teacher, so she can direct their attention to something new (Willis, 2006).

COMMUNICATION ISSUES

Research has shown that approximately 40 percent of the children with ASD are nonverbal. In addition, some children who are verbal do not use language in a functional manner. That means they may repeat the same phrase repeatedly or they may use echolalia, a term used to describe children who echo the same thing repeatedly. For example, when Sam's mother picks him up from school, she may ask, "What did you do today?" Sam may reply, "Time for circle!" repeatedly. It is important that children with autism develop a way to communicate with others. The most common forms of communication used by children with autism include

- Direct physical manipulation of a person or object. For example, taking a teacher's hand and pushing it toward a paintbrush to indicate "I want to paint" or giving a cup to a caregiver to indicate "more drink."
- Using gestures, such as pointing, showing, or a gaze shift (e.g., a child looks or points to a desired object and then shifts her gaze to another person, thereby indicating for the person to give her the desired object).
- Use of sounds, including crying, to communicate. In the extreme sense, a child might use a scream to indicate displeasure.
- Communication with a conventional sign language system. While it is difficult for many children with autism to understand the abstract nature of sign language, others have used it quite successfully.
- Picture systems, such as a two-dimensional photograph to communicate. Most children with autism relate better to real photographs than they do to abstract black-and-white drawings.

DEVELOPING SOCIAL SKILLS

Most children learn social skills through experience and observation. They watch how other children act and what other children do in social settings. Then, based on their observations, they imitate the behavior of others. Children with autism often lack the ability to learn social skills through observation or to interpret social cues from others. While typically developing children are likely to benefit from observing a social situation, a child with autism usually needs more cues. He must learn techniques that will help him respond appropriately in social settings. One technique that helps children with autism learn social skills is called social stories.

Social stories present appropriate social behaviors in the context of a story; Carol Gray developed this concept. Each story includes answers to questions, which people with autism need to know in order to interact with others. In other words, a social story answers who, what, when, where, and why questions about social interaction. In some senses, a social story can teach the child with autism to respond to others, even if she does not fully understand why she is doing so. By simply imitating what happened in the story in a real-life setting the child begins to experience some semblance of a social interaction with a peer. Social stories help the child with

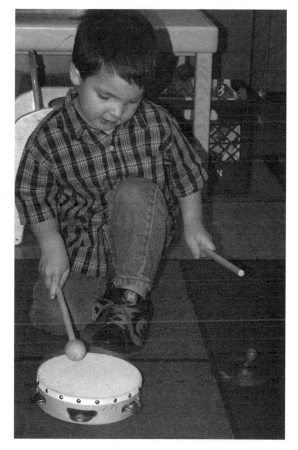

Figure 9.2   Children with Autism Spectrum Disorder (ASD) usually prefer solitary play.

autism learn to predict how others might act in a social situation, by giving her a better understanding of the thoughts, feelings, and point of view of other children. Social stories also help the child with autism learn more about what might be expected of her in such a setting (Gray, 2007).

SUMMARY

Children with autism will need an environment that is as well defined as possible. In addition, they will need a place within the classroom where they can go to be alone and "de-stress." This place should have indirect lighting, comfortable seating, and provide a sanctuary for the child to temporarily get away from sensory stimulation in the classroom. In addition, each center or learning area should be clearly marked with a picture. It is also very important that you include a picture schedule in each area, so the child can look at the schedule and get an idea of what is supposed to occur within that area. This should reduce anxiety and hopefully result in fewer outbursts. Remember, children with autism like to know what they are supposed to do, so a picture schedule is reassuring. In conclusion, children with autism function best when they have the following:

- structure and a predictable routine,
- environments that do not distract,
- verbal reminders of what will happen next,
- picture schedules to give them clues about what to do,
- a quiet place to go where they can be alone for a few minutes, and
- a classroom that does not overwhelm their senses with too much light and noise.

TERMS USED IN THIS CHAPTER

autism spectrum disorder (ASD)—also known as autism; this is a developmental disability that occurs in childhood and results in a combination of symptoms that include bizarre behaviors, issues with communication, social isolation, and difficulty with sensory integration. The symptoms vary from very severe to very mild.

communicative replacement—a behavior strategy in which a negative behavior is replaced with a more acceptable behavior.

disintegrative condition—a condition that worsens with time and results in losing previously learned skills or abilities.

echolalia—repeating the same phrase or word again and again.

functional behavior assessment—a method whereby the child's behavior is observed in an effort to determine the reasons for the behavior as well as the frequency and circumstances in which the behavior is observed.

ritualistic—a routine or activity that is done in the same manner, and often with repetition.

setting event—a specific event, which serves as a trigger for a behavior, such as forgetting to take medication, loss of sleep, illness, or change in temperature.

stereotypical behavior—a repetitive behavior pattern that serves no real functional purpose such as hand flapping.

RESOURCES USED IN THIS CHAPTER

American Psychiatric Association. (2000). *Diagnostic and statistical manual of mental disorders* (4th ed.). Washington, DC: Author.

Autism Information Center. (2007). *Frequently asked questions: Prevalence.* Retrieved December 1, 2007, from Autism Information Center: Centers for Disease Control and Prevention: http://www.cdc.gov/ncbddd/autism/faq_prevalence.htm

Gray, C. (2007). *What are social stories™?* Retrieved October 15, 2007, from The Gray Center for Social Learning and Understanding: http://www.thegraycenter.org

Parish-Morris, J., Hennon, E. A., Hirsh-Pasek, K., Golinkoff, R. M., & Tager-Flusberg, H. (2007). Children with autism illuminate the role of social intention in word learning. *Child Development 78*(4), 1265–1287.

Willis, C. (2006). *Teaching young children with autism spectrum disorder.* Beltsville, MD: Gryphon House.

Yale University Developmental Disabilities Clinic (n.d.). *Pervasive developmental delay not otherwise specified.* Retrieved November 27, 2007, from the Yale Developmental Disabilities Clinic, Yale University: http://www.med.yale.edu/chldstdy/autism/pddnos.html

SUGGESTED READING

Gray, C. (2000). *The new social story book.* Arlington, TX: Future Horizons Inc.

Hanbury, M. (2005). *Educating pupils with autistic spectrum disorders: A practical guide.* Thousand Oaks, CA: Paul Chapman Publishing.

Hoopmann, K. (2006). *All cats have Asperger's syndrome.* London, UK: Jessica Kingsley Publications.

Janzen, J. E. (2003). *Understanding the nature of autism: A guide to the autism spectrum disorders.* San Antonio, TX: Therapy Skill Builders.

Janzen, J. E. (1999). *Autism: Facts and strategies for parents.* San Antonio, TX: Therapy Skill Builders.

Kluth, P. (2003). *You're going to love this kid!: Teaching students with autism in the inclusive classroom.* Baltimore: Paul H. Brookes Publishing Co.

Wolfburg, P. J. (2003). *Peer play and the autism spectrum: The art of guiding children's socialization and imagination.* Shawnee Mission, KS: Autism Asperger Publishing Co.

THE RESEARCH SAYS . . .

The Role of Attention and Intention in Learning New Words

This research examined the extent with which children with autism (ASD) rely on attentional and intentional cues to learn new words. This process was then examined in typically developing children and the results compared for analysis. The research study consisted of four experiments in which 17 children with autism (*M* age = 5.08 years) were compared with 17 typically developing children (*M* ages = 2.57 to 3.12 years, respectively). The children were matched in terms of their mental age of functioning. The experiments compared the groups on nonverbal enactment and word-learning tasks. Results revealed variability in all groups, but particularly within the group with autism. Performance on tasks that required the child to understand the intent of a communication partner was the most powerful predictor of vocabulary in the group with autism. However, it was not a powerful predictor in the group of children without autism. The authors felt that these findings advanced the hypothesis that the ability to understand the intent of another plays a critical role in language acquisition. These findings suggest that word learning cannot be explained exclusively by either attentional or intentional processes, and they provide evidence of a special role for intentional understanding in the vocabulary development of children with autism. The authors did however, recognize that the sample size was small but felt the current research was a positive step toward a clearer understanding of the roles of social attention and word learning.

Parish-Morris, J., Hennon, E. A., Hirsh-Pasek, K., Golinkoff, R. M., & Tager-Flusberg, H. (2007). Children with autism illuminate the role of social intention in word learning. *Child Development 78*(4), 1265–1287.

Children With Sensory Processing Disorder

10

Figure 10.1   Children with Sensory Processing Disorder often
benefit from creative expression.

WHAT EXACTLY IS SENSORY INTEGRATION?

Almost 50 years ago, an occupational therapist named Jean Ayres described
a condition that resulted from an insufficient process in the brain in which
a person could not filter and process information received from their senses.
She used the term *sensory integration* (SI) *dysfunction* to describe a child who
is unable to analyze and respond appropriately to the information he
receives from his senses. SI is a process in which information is received
through our senses and sent to the brain to be organized (Kranowitz &

Miller, 2006). Most people develop the ability to filter out any unnecessary sensory information and respond appropriately to the environment. For example, when you walk into a grocery store, sensory integration gives you the ability to filter out the surrounding smells, noise, and light, so you can move around the store and select items you want to buy.

When asked to name their senses, most people respond with sight, hearing, touch, taste, and smell. What they do not realize is that there are two more senses that are equally important: *vestibular* (movement) and *proprioception* (awareness of body position).

Table 10.1   The Hidden Senses

Vestibular System	Proprioceptive System
Helps determine a sense of equilibrium, also referred to as balance	Orients the child, so she knows where her body is in space (upright, prone, etc.)
Responsible for eye-hand coordination or the way the eyes and hands work together to accomplish a motor task such as writing	Provides the central nervous system with information that affects the muscles and joints
Using both sides of the body to move such as when you walk or run	Allows the child to know distance such as how far it is from the table to the floor
Orientation of the head	Regulates the amount of pressure that is comfortable; for example, this system would alert a child if his shoes were too tight

SENSORY INTEGRATION DISORDER

When these hidden senses cannot work together to help regulate the nervous system and build the foundation for purposeful movement, the child may develop a sensory integration disorder. *SI dysfunction, SI disorder,* and *sensory modulation disorder* are terms used interchangeably to describe a condition in which children are unable to process the information that their senses receive in their brain. Many children with Autism Spectrum Disorder (ASD) have significant sensory integration issues. A child can have, however, a SI disorder that is not linked to a specific type of special need such as autism.

For a child with a sensory integration disorder, the normal noise in a busy early childhood classroom can be unbearably loud; the light from incandescent lights is more like a spotlight than an overhead light. As you observe children in your classroom, you will be able to determine which children have issues with sensory integration (Isbell & Isbell, 2007).

You should be aware of two types of SI disorders: hypersensitive (over-stimulated by sensory information) and hyposensitive (understimulated by sensory information). Hypersensitive children may cover their ears when they hear a noise or hide their eyes when it is too bright. Hyposensitive children seem to be in "another world" where they cannot see, hear, feel, or touch anything at all. Hyposensitive children are at a much greater risk for getting hurt than are hypersensitive children. Because they do not often respond to sound, they may walk in front of a moving bus, pick up a hot skillet, or get to the top of a staircase and fall to the bottom. Table 10.2 provides some guidelines for how to determine if a child is hyposensitive or hypersensitive.

Table 10.2 Sensory Responses to Everyday Stimuli

Sense	Oversensitive (Hypersensitive)	Undersensitive (Hyposensitive)
Vision (sight)	• Covers his eyes when the lights are too bright • Upset when pictures are too colorful • Squints or rubs his eyes frequently	• Appears as though she has a vision loss, in that she does not respond to light • Holds items too close to look at them • Stares at flickering fluorescent lights
Sound	• Covers his ears at the slightest noise • Responds to sounds other children ignore such as the hum of an air-conditioner • Will act as though she cannot hear when you call her by name, but then responds when a child drops a toy	• Speaks loudly • Sings loudly • Always plays with toys that make loud noises • Plays music or the television too loudly
Smell	• Holds his nose at common odors • Sniffs the air or other people	• Ignores bad odors • May sniff people or toys • Does not respond to strong odors
Touch (Tactile)	• Gets upset when touched • Very sensitive to textures and materials • Opposed to getting dirty or touching things like finger paint • Scratches at her skin or startles when something touches her	• Bumps into people • Chews on items frequently • Unaware of temperature changes, will go outside without a coat or gloves • Seemingly unable to tell when he is in pain or injured • Does not cry when he falls down

(Continued)

Table 10.2 (Continued)

Sense	Oversensitive (Hypersensitive)	Undersensitive (Hyposensitive)
Taste	• Gags when he eats • Eats foods of only a certain texture • Sensitive to hot or cold foods	• Wants only spicy food • Adds a lot of pepper or salt to food • Licks objects or toys
Movement	• Does not like to move, dance, climb, or hop • Sways • Seems to walk "off-balance"	• Does not get dizzy when she whirls or turns around • Loves to move fast • In constant motion • Rocks • Moves her body all the time

Adapted from Willis, C. (2006). *Teaching young children with autism spectrum disorder (ASD)*. Beltsville, MD: Gryphon House.

WHAT CAN I DO TO MAKE MY CLASSROOM SENSORY "FRIENDLY"?

According to Kranowitz and Miller (2006), authors of the bestselling book *The Out-of-Sync Child*, "Just as the five main food groups provide daily nutritional requirements, a daily sensory diet fulfills physical and emotional needs" (p. 20). An SI diet includes a combination of alerting, organizing, and calming techniques that help the child with sensory issues cope with all the input he receives. An occupational therapist (OT) is an excellent resource to help you learn how to organize the environment in your classroom in a way that is "sensory friendly."

These guidelines may help in determining what you can do to create an environment that meets the sensory needs of children with sensory processing issues. First, look for activities that are stimulating for children who are undersensitive to sensory input. These activities include such things as combining music and movement to dance around the room, bouncing on a ball, or jumping up and down. It is useful to play games that involve smell such as "Guess the Smell," where a child is blindfolded and asked to smell an object in an effort to determine what it is, and to eat foods that crunch such as celery, popcorn, or pretzel sticks. For a child who is undersensitive or is an underresponder to sensory input, try to combine movements into daily routines as much as possible. For example, transition to a new activity by jumping like a kangaroo or hopping like a rabbit.

Organizing activities are opportunities for the child to develop self-awareness by learning to organize her feelings. This often means having a quiet place to go for a few minutes to "de-stress" or to take a break from the bombardment of sound-, smell-, touch-, and sight-based activities that take place during a normal school day. Every classroom should have a "quiet center." Children can go to this place that is "sensory safe" and that provides soft lighting, comfortable seating, and refuge from daily routines. It is not time-out or a place for the teacher to send overactive children. Rather, it is a place that the child chooses to go for a few minutes. It is very important, however, that all children, especially those with special needs, learn that the "quiet center" is available when they need it, but it is not a place to go to avoid partici-

Figure 10.2 Children with Sensory Processing Disorder respond to materials designed for their sensory needs.

pation in activities for a lengthy period. The rule should always be that upon returning from the quiet center, a child must continue with the activity she was participating in prior to going to the quiet center. Children learn very quickly how to manipulate the environment in an effort to avoid altogether an undesirable activity.

Children with SI disorders sometimes respond well to items that enable them to better organize all the input they receive through their senses. These items, referred to as "calmers," include

- "chewies"—things the child can chew on such as commercially purchased plastic tubing;
- weighted vests—vests with a little "weight" sewn into the pockets;
- "squeeze" toys—soft things that can be squeezed;
- soft seats—seating such as beanbag chairs or therapy balls to sit on; and
- body cocoons—stretchy material for children to wrap themselves into.

One of the most important things you can do to make your classroom sensory friendly is to determine if the light in the classroom is too bright. Florescent lights can be especially distracting for children with SI issues. Look for ways you can use indirect lighting such as lamps or, at the very least, nonflorescent overhead lights.

Regulate the environmental noise so that it is not so loud that a child is unable to function. Watch for signs that the child is being overwhelmed by noise in the classroom. This may be indicated if he begins to look nervously around the room, begins fidgeting, or cov-

Figure 10.3   Follow the child's lead.

ers his ears with his hands. Provide a quiet place for the child to go to desensitize and get away from the noise.

Be aware of the smells in your classroom. To you, the sweet smell of strawberry-scented air fresher might be pleasing and enhance your classroom. It may interfere, however, with the learning ability of a child with SI disorder. If you use scents in the classroom, use natural ones, and then only after you have determined that the child can tolerate them. For example, you might try peppermint, lavender, or vanilla, instead of sweet, flowery scents.

MATERIALS FOR THE "SENSORY FRIENDLY" CLASSROOM

Fine motor skills are critically important for future writing success. For a child who might be tactilely sensitive, it is important to provide a variety of writing materials such as chubby crayons, colored pencils with pencil grips, and glue; various art materials such as construction paper, cloth, and ribbon; and puzzles with knobs. In addition, encourage children to use materials such as Legos™; Wikki sticks; sandpaper; child-size tools such as a hammer and nails; toys that light up and make noise; and games that encourage movement such as rocking or dancing (see Table 10.3).

Table 10.3 Suggestions for Sensory Integration

Sensory Area	Activities
Auditory	**Oversensitive:** Provide headphones for listening to music, as the oversensitive child will have a tendency to play music too loud. Play games that distinguish inside voices from outside voices. Provide toys and art materials that make noise such as sandpaper, bubble wrap, and Styrofoam.
	Undersensitive: Sit the undersensitive child next to you for circle time. Ask the child questions about things that interest her. Change sounds when possible and play games where you play a sound on an audio player and the child tries to guess what object made the sound.
Visual	**Oversensitive:** Keep lighting soft and "glare-free" whenever possible. Allow the child to wear sunglasses if it makes it easier for him to function. Encourage the child to take a break, close his eyes, and relax.
	Undersensitive: Play games where the child has to make eye contact with you. Provide opportunities for visual stimulation such as looking at artwork and talking about what you see, drawing pictures using vivid colors, and identifying words and letters in the environment.
Taste/Smell	**Oversensitive:** Encourage the child to smell new things but recognize that some smells will be too much for the child. Avoid using scented air-fresheners, crayons, and scent machines in the classroom.
	Undersensitive: Explore scents and smells, go for a nature walk, talk about what you smell, and play games where you ask the child to "name that smell."
Body Position	**Oversensitive:** The child may be calmed by a weighted blanket, weighted vest, or wrist weights. Do not use weighted backpacks, as these can actually harm the child.
	Undersensitive: Roll the child in a blanket, invite the child to help hold up the wall in the classroom by pushing against it, use deep pressure such as tight hugs, carrying an armload of blocks, or opening a heavy door.
Movement	**Oversensitive:** Swing on swings, varying the types of swings and the movements, such as front and back and side-to-side. Spin on a *Sit n' Spin* or *Dizzy Disc, Jr.*, run in a circle, ride a carousel, or dance in a circle with a brightly colored scarf.
	Undersensitive: Get the child to bounce around like a rabbit. Invite the child to pick a friend and play "Simon Says" with movement.

(Continued)

Table 10.3   (Continued)

Sensory Area	Activities
Touch	**Oversensitive:** Attempt to get the child to eat foods that will provide sensations in the mouth such as bubbles from carbonated beverages. Play with foamy soap or shaving cream (add sand for extra texture), use finger-paint, play with glitter glue, and use clay and Play-Doh for art. If your regulations allow, fill a tub with dry beans and rice or other materials and hide some objects inside the mixture. Go for a treasure hunt. Do not force a child who is unwilling to touch all these "messy" substances. Let her use a paintbrush, if she prefers.
	Undersensitive: The child may always cling to others and have very little regard for personal space. Provide opportunities to learn about personal space and provide items such as "chewies" for the child to chew on during the day. Provide lots of different textures for the child to feel and touch throughout the day. The child will enjoy the traditional "feely box" and have no problem sticking her hand inside to feel what is hidden there.

TERMS USED IN THIS CHAPTER

proprioception—the process that orients the child so he knows where his body is in space (upright, prone, etc.)

sensory integration diet—includes a combination of alerting, organizing, and calming techniques that help the child with sensory issues cope with all the input she receives

sensory integration disorder—also called sensory integration dysfunction, when the brain has difficulty processing information received from the senses

sensory integration (SI)—the process by which the senses work together to help organize the information received by the brain

vestibular—the ability to coordinate movement

RESOURCES USED IN THIS CHAPTER

Atchison, B. J. (2007). Sensory modulation disorders among children with a history of trauma: A frame of reference for speech language pathologists. *Language, speech and hearing services in schools, 38*(2), 106–116.

Isbell, C., & Isbell, R. (2007). *Sensory integration: A guide for preschool teachers.* Beltsville, MD: Gryphon House.

Kranowitz, C., & Miller, L. J. (2006). *The out-of-sync child: Recognizing and coping with sensory processing disorder* (Rev. ed.). New York: Perigee Trade.

Willis, C. (2006). *Teaching young children with autism spectrum disorder.* Beltsville, MD: Gryphon House.

SUGGESTED READING

Beil, L., & Peske, N. (2005). *Raising a sensory smart child: The definitive book for helping your child with sensory integration issues.* New York: Penguin.

Heilberger, D. W., & Heiniger-White, M. C. (2000). *S'cool moves for learning: A program designed to enhance learning through body-mind integration.* Reading, CA: Integrated Learning Press.

Heller, S. (2003). *It's too loud, too fast, too tight, too bright: What to do if you are sensory defensive in an over stimulating world.* New York: Harper.

Kranowitz, C. (2003). *The out-of-sync child has fun: Activities for kids with sensory integration dysfunction.* New York: Perigee Trade.

Smith, K. A. (2004). *The sensory-sensitive child: Practical solutions for out-of-bounds behavior.* New York: Collins.

THE RESEARCH SAYS . . .

Trauma and Sensory Modulation Disorder

The author presented definitions and concepts about sensory modulation and sensory modulation disorders in the context of research conducted on children with a history of trauma who were clients at Southwest Michigan Children's Trauma Assessment Center (CTAC). The author described behavioral aspects of sensory modulation disorders, described a framework for assessment, and discussed the disorder in terms of current research. After a literature review, the author examined the impact of exposure to both prenatal and postnatal trauma on sensory modulation. The review of the literature indicates support for the presence of sensory modulation disorders among traumatized children. In addition, the emerging data now being gathered on children who have been assessed by CTAC indicate a significant prevalence of sensory modulation disorders among children with a history of trauma alone, and those with both trauma and a diagnosis of fetal alcohol spectrum disorder (FASD). The author proposes that for intervention services and treatment to be successful, professionals must be aware of behaviors associated with this disorder. Sensory modulation is a desired state of emotional and physical well-being. According to the author, "all humans intermittently experience physical and emotional stress, illness, trauma, and other events that create a discomfit between our internal selves and the external world. The need for adaptation—to flee or fight—is a natural human response, and the ability to adapt prevents a disregulated state." He concludes that professionals need a better understanding of how sensory modulation disorders impact the human adaptive process. The author feels that technology such as functional magnetic resonance imaging (f MRI) will enable researchers to be more precise in determining the location of brain changes and, therefore, to become better suited to deal with the impact of trauma on sensory modulation.

Atchison, B. J. (2007). Sensory modulation disorders among children with a history of trauma: A frame of reference for speech language pathologists. *Language, Speech and Hearing Services in Schools, 38*(2), 106–116.

Children At Risk 11 for School Failure

Figure 11.1   Look for opportunities for children in foster care to build self-esteem.

WHO ARE CHILDREN AT RISK?

In general, at risk is used to describe children who are either living in or exposed to situations that limit the likelihood of their success in school. These situations include

- extreme poverty,
- homelessness,
- family factors (adolescent mothers, incarcerated parents, foster care),
- chronic illness, and
- development of a future learning disability.

Children who are considered at risk will need additional support in order to be successful in school. Support might include additional literacy and preliteracy instruction, more opportunities to develop social skills and social interaction skills, additional help in developing language, and learning to manage challenging behaviors.

CHILDREN LIVING IN EXTREME POVERTY

According to the Children's Defense Fund, an organization dedicated to advocating for children, extreme poverty refers to children living at less than one-half of the poverty level. While there are many ways to define poverty, generally speaking, it refers to the lowest 10 percent of the population in per-capita income. However, many subtle factors influence poverty. For example, poverty depends on the number of family members or dependents in the household and the number of wage earners. Extreme poverty would then be those children whose family is at the lower end of the poverty scale. To put this into context, it would mean that a family in extreme poverty would have to live on less than $20 per day. Surprisingly, 70 percent of the children living in extreme poverty have at least one family member who works full time (Children's Defense Fund, 2005). A disproportionate number of these children are children of color and children who have one or more family members who do not speak English. In addition to being at risk for school failure, children from extremely poor homes often do not receive proper medical care and are more likely to have experienced both hunger and homelessness than their peers. Also, children who live in extreme poverty are more likely than their peers to be victims of physical abuse, witness violent crimes, and have a parent who is incarcerated. By the time they reach preschool, a child who lives in extreme poverty may have developed

- challenging behaviors,
- a poor self-esteem,
- a lack of understanding of how to interact with others,
- limited language skills, and
- a lack of opportunities to be exposed to early literacy activities.

HOMELESSNESS

Within the past few years, a new definition of homelessness has emerged. Today, a child is considered homeless if he does not have a permanent address. This definition includes children who move from relative to relative—staying for a few weeks with one relative and staying a few weeks or months with another. In addition, it includes a child who lives continuously in a car, a homeless shelter, or, worse, in an open environment, such as under a bridge or in an abandoned building. In addition, homeless children usually live in families with multiple young children. Because these children do not have the opportunity to interact with toys and books, they may come into your class not knowing what to do or how to respond.

According to the National Child Traumatic Stress Network (2004), children who are homeless

- often live with mothers who have experienced physical or sexual assault themselves;
- are twice as likely to get sick as other children;
- go hungry twice as often as nonhomeless children;
- usually lack personal possessions;
- have twice the rate of learning disabilities as their peers; and
- are much more likely to develop anxiety, depression, or withdrawal.

FAMILY FACTORS

Children of adolescent mothers are at a higher risk than their peers of developing delays that result in problems in academic success (Whitman, Borkowski, Schellenbach, & Nath, 1997; Brooks-Gunn & Furstenburg, 1986; Black et al., 2004). Statistics show that teen mothers are less likely to receive prenatal care and often have children who are born prematurely (Moore, Morrison, & Greene, 1997). In addition, adolescent mothers have the added stress of dealing with an unplanned or unwanted pregnancy. For this reason, children of adolescent mothers are at a high risk of abuse and neglect (George & Lee, 1997). These factors contribute to the probability of the child having issues with attachment (Schwartz, McRoy, & Downs, 2004).

Children of incarcerated parents deal with unique issues, such as not being able to see their parents very often, experiencing trauma at the time their parent was arrested, and being placed in foster care or with relatives who are already living in poverty or in a high-stress environment themselves (Benedict, Zuravin, & Stallings, 1996). In 2006, the Council on Crime and Justice described children of incarcerated parents as stigmatized and having issues with bonding, attachment, social skills, behaviors, and learning. In addition, well-meaning caretakers may attempt to protect the child by saying things like, "Dad is working far away," "Mom is in the hospital," or ". . . away at school" (Nesmith, Ruhland, & Krueger,

2006). Research has found that not telling children the truth can have a negative impact and result in the child not trusting any adult (Adalist-Estrin, n.d.).

Children in foster care may not only have attachment issues but also are often placed in foster care for reasons such as sexual abuse, chronic neglect, or physical abuse. They frequently have issues relating to others, trusting adults, understanding appropriate touching of others, and knowing how to interact with other children (Harden, 2004). Because the nature of their lives is transient, they often lack personal possessions and have trouble with anxiety and maintaining social relationships. The American Academy of Pediatrics (2000) describes some of the developmental issues related to children in foster care such as the implications and consequences of abuse and neglect on early brain development, the challenges of establishing attachment to a caregiver, and the child's response to stress.

CHRONIC ILLNESS

Children with chronic illness are at greater risk for developing emotional problems than their peers. Coping with the knowledge that a child's illness may not be temporary, and in fact could get worse, adds additional stress to the family as a whole. Since young children sometimes have difficulty understanding the reality of a chronic illness, they might feel they are being "punished" for some imagined bad behavior. The child may react negatively to being pampered, being told she cannot participate in a given activity, or having to endure lengthy and sometimes painful medical treatments for her condition.

Because the chronically ill child will miss school often, he subsequently does not make the same academic progress as his peers, has fewer opportunities to develop lasting social relationships and friendships, and feels isolated and alone much of the time. Since family members may have had to protect the child from other illnesses and limit his social contact with others, the child may have difficulty separating from family members and may act afraid of new environments and new people. Mental health issues are common in children with chronic illness, especially depression and anxiety disorders (Martini, 2007).

FUTURE LEARNING DISABILITY

Learning disabilities are normally not identified until a child has had the opportunity to receive several years of direct instruction in content areas such as reading or math. This concept of waiting until the child has developed a deficit, often around the third or fourth grade, is referred to as a discrepancy model. In a discrepancy model, the child's school waits until the gaps between her learning and those of her peers are significant before offering specific interventions. Many educators believe that if we intervene earlier, the likelihood of a learning disability may be diminished significantly. Techniques, such as Response to Intervention (RTI), are employed early, so the child's needs are met sooner rather than later. For a full discussion of RTI, see Chapter 14. Learning disabilities are often grouped into three categories: speech or language disorders; problems with reading and/or writing, and math skills. Needless to say, instruction in these skills is not considered developmentally appropriate for young children. However, the Coordinated Campaign for Learning Disabilities (1997) provides a list of "red flags" that may be indicative of a future learning problem. These include

- attention deficit disorders,
- delayed speech,
- pronunciation problems,
- difficulty learning new words,
- difficulty learning to read,
- trouble learning numbers or the alphabet,
- short attention span,
- difficulty following directions, and
- poor grasp of a crayon or pen.

CLASSROOM SUGGESTIONS FOR CHILDREN AT RISK

Table 11.1   Suggestions for the Classroom

At-Risk Condition	*Classroom Modifications Specific to At-Risk Conditions*
Extreme Poverty	• Look for opportunities that build self-esteem. • Whenever possible, provide extra snacks. • Establish a relationship with the family and try to help them access community resources, especially free health care clinics and job training opportunities. • Provide suggestions for no-cost activities families can do together to build literacy skills.
Homelessness	• Keep rules simple, but enforce them consistently. • Provide additional opportunities for the child to interact with novel toys, art activities, books, music, and computers. • Model appropriate activities for making and keeping friends.

(Continued)

Table 11.1 (Continued)

At-Risk Condition	Classroom Modifications Specific to At-Risk Conditions
Adolescent Mother	• Encourage the child's mother to participate in parenting classes, access local community resources, and return to school, when applicable. • Develop rapport without making judgments about the child's home environment. • Provide additional opportunities for the child to learn and develop her vocabulary. • Read stories to the children that encourage acceptance of others.
Incarcerated Parent	• Look for volunteers to be a role model for the child (retired persons, college students, community leaders). • Allow the child to discuss his feelings. • Model tolerance and acceptance in the classroom. • Involve the child in activities that make him feel special and unique.
Foster Care	• Find opportunities to place the child in leadership roles and compliment her on her successes. • Encourage friendships with others. • Avoid talking about the circumstances that caused the child to be placed in foster care, unless specifically advised to do so by a trained professional. • Recognize that the child may be suspicious of adults and have a difficult time trusting them. It is very important that she learns to recognize that you can be trusted. • Look for ways to give the child books, art materials, etc., that she can keep for herself.
Chronic Illness	• When the child is at school, try to pair him with others who have similar interests. • Establish a relationship with the family, so that they are aware of what the class is doing when the child is absent. • If the family is willing, talk to the child about his illness and answer his questions as honestly as possible. • Build on the child's strengths and praise him when he learns a new skill.
Learning Disability	• Try to identify how the child learns (visual, auditory, etc.) and look for ways to present information in that mode. • Recognize that the child may need additional practice to learn new concepts and master new skills. • Use computer programs and one-on-one instruction to help the child with aspects of literacy or math that are especially problematic for her. • Try to identify her strengths and build her self-esteem in ways that encourage her to keep trying.

TERMS USED IN THIS CHAPTER

chronic illness—children with long-term illnesses that affect the activities in which they are able to participate.

discrepancy model—the traditional model used to diagnose learning disabilities in which evaluation and determinations are made after the child performs significantly behind his peers in a content area of instruction.

homelessness—having no home or the lack of a fixed place to live (i.e., anyone whose day-to-day living arrangements are precarious).

poverty level—generally defined as the lowest 10% of the population, based on per capita income.

RESOURCES USED IN THIS CHAPTER

Adalist-Estrin, A. (n.d.). Questions children ask. *Children of prisoners library: Facts and issues.* CPL 103.

American Academy of Pediatrics: Committee on Early Childhood, Adoption, and Dependent Care. (2000). Developmental issues for young children in foster care. *Pediatrics, 106*(5), 1145–1150.

Benedict, M. I., Zuravin, S., & Stallings, R. Y. (1996). Adult functioning of children who lived in kin versus nonrelative family foster home. *Child Welfare 75*(X), 529–549.

Black, M. M., Papa, M. A., Hussey, J. M., Hunter, W., Dubowitz, H., Kotch, J. B., English, D., & Schneider, M. (2002). Behavior and development of preschool children born to adolescent mothers: Risk and 3 generation households. *Pediatrics 109*(4), 573–580.

Brooks-Gunn, J., & Furstenberg, F. F. (1986). The children of adolescent mothers: Physical, academic, and psychological outcomes. *Developmental Review, 6,* 224–251.

Children's Defense Fund. (2005). *Federal poverty levels for 2004.* Washington, DC: Author.

Coordinated Campaign for Learning Disabilities. (1997, April). *Early Warning Signs of Learning Disabilities.* Retrieved September 1, 2007, from http://www.ldonline.org/article/226

George, R. M., & Lee, B. J. (1997). Abuse and neglect of children. In R. Maynard (Ed.), *Kids having kids* (205–230). Washington, DC: The Urban Institute Press.

Harden, B. J. (2004). Safety and Stability for Foster Children: A Developmental Perspective. *Children, families and foster care, 13*(1), 31–47.

Martini, R. D. (2007). *Helping children cope with chronic illness.* American Academy of Child and Adolescent Psychiatry. Retrieved August 13, 2007, from http://www.aacap.org/cs/root/developmentor/helping_children_cope_with_chronic_illness

Moore, K. A., Morrison, D. R., & Greene, A. D. (1997). Effects on children born to adolescent mothers. In R. Maynard (Ed.), *Kids having kids* (145–180). Washington DC: The Urban Institute Press.

National Child Traumatic Stress Network. (2004). *Facts on traumatic stress and children with developmental disabilities.* Los Angeles, CA: National Center for Child Traumatic Stress.

Nesmith, A., Ruhland, E., & Krueger, S. (2006). *Children of incarcerated parents.* Minneapolis, MN: Council on Crime and Justice.

Schwartz, A. E., McRoy, R. G., & Downs, A. C. (2004). Adolescent mothers in a transitional living facility: An exploratory study of support networks and attachment patterns. *Journal of Adolescent Research, 19*(1), 85–112.

Whitman, T. L., Borkowski, J. G., Schellenbach, C. J., & Nath, P. S. (1997). Predicting and understanding developmental delay of children of adolescent mothers: A multidimensional approach. *American Journal of Mental Deficiency, 92*(1), 40–56.

SUGGESTED READING

Garguilo, R. M. (2006). Homeless and disabled rights, responsibilities and recommendations for serving young children with special needs. *Early Childhood Education Journal, 33*(5), 357–362.

Hairston, C. F., Rollin J., & Jo, H. (2004). Family connections during imprisonment and prisoners' community reentry. *Research brief: Children, families, and the criminal justice system.* Chicago: University of Illinois.

Kainz, K., & Vernon-Feagans, L. (2007). The ecology of early reading development for children in poverty, *Elementary School Journal, 107*(5), 407–427.

Sullivan, P., & Knutson, J. (2000). Maltreatment and disabilities: A population-based epidemiological study. *Child Abuse and Neglect, 24*(10), 1257–1273.

THE RESEARCH SAYS . . .

Teen Mothers Living in Transitional Shelters Need Support

Much of the current research on adolescent mothers has dealt primarily with young mothers living in a family environment. Schwarts, McRoy, and Downs (2004) examined 25 teen mothers living in a transitional facility. While this is a relatively small sample size, their conclusions are still relevant to the issues faced by these young mothers. They examined how the mothers involved in the study formed attachments to four groups: their parents, their romantic partners, their children, and the program staff at the facility in which they were living. Researchers also attempted to identify the possible outcomes for the children of these adolescent mothers, related to the type of bonding that had formed between the mother and child. They found that most of the participants in their study had tremendous challenges forming attachments with adults and with their own children. As a result, researchers recommended that staff at transitional shelters receive extra training in how to help adolescent mothers form positive attachments. The authors concluded that, based on the mothers' lack of positive emotionally healthy attachments, it would consequently reflect negatively in their future relationships with their own children. Without intervention, this in turn would have long-term effects on how the children of these adolescent mothers would form secure attachments themselves.

Schwartz, A. E., McRoy, R. G., & Downs, A. C. (2004). Adolescent mothers in a transitional living facility: An exploratory study of support networks and attachment patterns. *Journal of Adolescent Research, 19*(1), 85–112.

Part III

Strategies for the Inclusive Classroom

Preparing the Children

12

Figure 12.1   Provide materials that help children build motor skills.

BEFORE THE FIRST DAY OF SCHOOL

Being prepared for an inclusive or blended classroom can be a daunting task. However, with a little careful planning, it can be an experience that is meaningful for you and, most important, for the children in your classroom. It is important that you do some preliminary research, so that you know as much as possible about the children with special needs who will be members of your classroom community. While reading their "official school files" is very important, you are more likely to get to know the child if you meet her and her family prior to the first day of school. The extra hour you invest in interviewing families and other caregivers, in combination with giving the child an opportunity to explore her new classroom, will pay off in many positive ways.

Children with special needs generally tend to be fearful of new settings, people, and routines. A "tour" prior to school starting is an ideal way to help the child become more familiar with his new environment. Invite the child and his family to visit your classroom. When he arrives, speak to him by name and welcome him, but keep in mind, many children are naturally shy around people they do not know. Talk to his family about his needs and his strengths, as well as his weaknesses. Ask about things that are challenging for him, such as toileting issues, or sitting in a large group. Some questions you will want to ask the child and/or his family when they visit your classroom include:

1. What are his favorite activities at home?
2. Is there something he is particularly "fearful" about?
3. What are his favorite foods? Does he have any food "jags"?
4. What are his favorite toys? Cartoon figures?
5. Who does he interact or play with at home?
6. Does he have any pets? What are their names?
7. Does he have any allergies that you should know about?
8. What is his favorite color? Does he have a book that he enjoys?
9. Has he been with other children before? Are there other siblings at home?
10. Who are the other adults in his world (caretakers, afterschool caregivers, and family members who spend time with him)?
11. What is the family's main goal for him during the coming school year?
12. Are there safety issues you need to be aware of? (For example, some children are prone to running away or hiding when they are frightened.)

Invite the child and his family to walk with you around the classroom. Point out various learning centers. Follow the child's lead; if he stops and looks at a particular center, give him a few minutes to explore it independently. Remember, children with special needs often require a few extra minutes to process new information. Tell the child a few things about what he will be doing at school, but be cautious not to overwhelm him with too much information. The idea of the initial visit is to give him time to see his new environment without other children present.

Begin establishing rapport with the child and her family by assuring them that you are looking forward to working with them and that you want this to be a positive experience for everyone. Establish a pattern of talking about the child's strengths as well as her challenges. If possible, explain to the family that you would like permission to answer questions about their child that other children in the class might ask. Assure them that you will always answer questions in a manner that respects the child and that your intention is to help other children focus on ways their child can be involved in classroom activities.

Before the family leaves, make sure there is a method established for communication. For example, a notebook could be sent home every night with comments about what the child did that day and a family member could write notes to you as well. Other ways to communicate regularly include e-mail or a special mailbox where you and the family can exchange notes and messages.

HOW DO I PREPARE CHILDREN IN A GENERAL EDUCATION SETTING FOR A CHILD WITH SPECIAL NEEDS?

Young children are naturally curious and ask many questions. Most questions about children with special needs are asked by other children who are curious. It is common for any child to be naturally curious when he sees something or someone who is different. Usually, once you answer the question, the child is satisfied and quickly moves on to something else. Nevertheless, you need to be prepared to answer questions, such as, "Why is he in a wheelchair?" or "Doesn't Laquisha talk?"

In addition, you should expect some children to make comments about the child that are negative or derogatory. For example, "Bobby gets away with breaking the rules—that's not fair!" or "He talks funny." There is always the possibility that someone may say something hurtful like, "He's stupid," or "She's a baby—she wets her pants." These questions and comments should be addressed in a different manner than questions asked by a child who is simply curious about his classmate with special needs. It is very important that you establish and maintain an absolute rule that derogatory or demeaning comments are not tolerated. A child who makes these kinds of comments is not learning tolerance and understanding of others. Take the child to a quiet place where you can talk one-on-one. Begin the conversation by reminding her that friends don't say things to hurt each other. Talk about strengths and weaknesses, and see if the child will rephrase her question or response in a manner that is more in keeping with how we treat each other. In addition, it is important for the child to see by your demeanor and facial expressions that you are displeased with her remarks. The more often you model tolerance and acceptance, and talk about respecting each other and respecting differences, the more likely questions and comments like those mentioned above will decrease.

WHAT KINDS OF ACTIVITIES TEACH TOLERANCE AND ACCEPTANCE OF OTHERS?

Children are naturally more tolerant of others when they feel a sense of community and when they recognize that each member of the community is an equal partner. To accomplish this, you will need to establish an environment that is both independent (children have opportunities to make choices and function as individuals) and interdependent (working together for the whole community). This balance between the child as an individual and the child as part of a group is not easy, but it is vital if the child is going to grow into an emotionally healthy adult.

Children are also more tolerant of others when they understand and practice the basic tenets of making and keeping a friend. Building emotional health through friendship skills should be as much a part of the early childhood curriculum as literacy and number skills. Just telling children to "act friendly" or saying, "Friends don't hit each other," is meaningless. Instead, comment on specific friendship skills that you observe during an ordinary day. Examples are shown in Table 12.1.

Table 12.1   Building Friendship Skills

Friendship Skill	*Teacher Comment*
Playing together	Ashley and Peter are building a boat together in the block area. Sandra and Kisha are setting the table together in home living.
Helping each other	Thank you, Arliss, for helping Irving get his snack. Devon, I appreciate the way you helped Kevin reach the paintbrushes.
Being polite	Deb, great job remembering to say please when you asked Jabron to hand you a puzzle. Juan, you always remember to say thank you when I give you more milk at lunch.

Sharing	Corky shares his Legos™ with Davis when they build.
	Darlene, you do such a nice job of sharing the paints with Cameron.
Understanding the feelings of others	Petra, thanks for sitting so quietly when Amber fell down. It gave me more time to help her feel better.
	Curtis, thank you for telling me Kara was crying. You really understand when she gets upset.
Seeing another person's point of view	Arabella, you and Sam both wanted to be on the computer. I appreciate you letting him go first.
	Candice, I know you like to be the line leader, but letting Maria be first was a nice thing to do.

Keep in mind that children with special needs will need additional assistance and modeling in order to learn the friendship skills listed. Look for opportunities to help them role-play how friends treat each other, and use gestures and cues as reminders. For example, if a child with special needs always interrupts when you are talking to another child, look at her, bring your finger to your lips, shake your head no, and continue talking with the first child. When you are finished, direct your attention to the child with special needs. Do not forget to praise her for waiting until it was her turn to talk to you. Select specific skills to work on and send home notes encouraging family members to reinforce those skills at home. When a child does an especially good job of being a friend or using an important social skill, send a note of congratulations home. An example of one is provided below:

> Just a little note to say your child, _____,
>
> did really great today!
>
> I am so proud and happy too,
>
> to share this good news with you!
>
> Thank her/him once again for me,
>
> for treating others considerately.

THE SOCIALLY COMPETENT CHILD

Much has been written about the socially competent child in an early childhood setting. Social competence, or the ability to be confident and independent in a social setting, is especially difficult for children with special needs. Some ideas to help a child with special needs become more socially competent include:

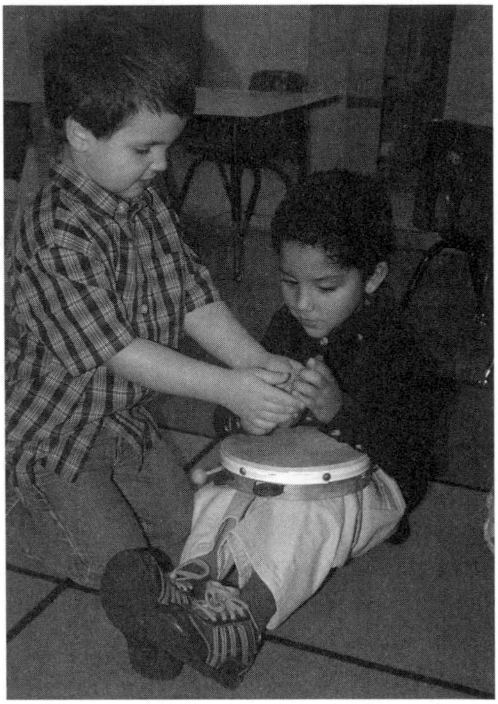

Figure 12.2 Look for opportunities that enable children with special needs to partially participate.

1. Encourage peers to work together by setting up collaboration activities. For a child who is reluctant to work in a group, you may want to select a "peer helper" to work or play with the child.

2. Offer opportunities for making choices. This gives the child some control over his environment. Never provide more than two choices, as it may be too confusing.

3. Give the child assigned tasks to do. If she cannot complete a whole task, try having her job share with a peer. For example, one child might hold a trashcan, while another child lifts out the trash bag and replaces it. This is called partial participation—the child takes part in an activity, even if she is unable to complete the task independently.

4. Use praise frequently. Tell him you are proud of him for trying. Think of ways to let his family know that he is trying new tasks, even if he has not mastered them yet.

5. Show children how to greet each other by modeling how to greet others, using phrases such as "good morning" and "goodbye." Ask questions that show the child you are interested in what she is doing.

6. Remind children that they are always to use soft touches and words, not fists. Read books that emphasize how children should treat each other, such as *Hands Are Not for Hitting* by Martine Agassi.

7. Teach children how to wait. Practice taking turns and let the child see that waiting for his turn is often necessary.

Strategy

Selecting a Peer Helper to Model Social Skills

Purpose: The purpose of this strategy is to enable children with special needs to interact with a peer buddy who will play or work with them on a designated activity.

Focus: Explain to the peer you have selected that you are inviting her to be a peer helper for _____ (use the child's name), and that her role as "peer buddy" is just for this activity. Tell the child how pleased you are that she has decided to help.

Develop:
1. Consider the maturity level and communication skills of each child before pairing them up.
2. Insure that the peer buddy knows about the specific strengths and weaknesses of the child with special needs. Make sure the buddy knows how the child with special needs communicates with others.
3. When the two children interact for the first time, watch carefully for any challenges that you may have overlooked.
4. Encourage the peer buddy to greet the child by name, and invite (but don't force) the child to join in an activity with her. Tell the peer buddy to talk to the child, even if the child is unable to communicate with her. Encourage her to describe the activity and wait before doing something for the peer with disabilities that he can do for himself.

Practice:
1. Practice in class, and remember that it may be necessary to model for both buddies. Illustrate what you want them to do or how you want them to behave.
2. Start buddy sessions during an unstructured time such as snack time and/or free choice time. Start with four to six minutes and work up to longer periods.
3. Encourage the relationship through positive support.
4. Keep in mind that relationships take time; the goal of this activity is to help both children learn to be friends.

5. When you observe that enjoyable interactions between children are occurring, expand to a more structured activity.

6. As the children become more comfortable with each other, you may have to remind them less frequently about the rules of social interaction.

Reflect:

1. If one peer buddy does not work out, do not give up—try another child.

Figure 12.3 Children interact in the Take-Apart Center.

2. Think about what worked and what did not work.

Table 12.2 Ideas for Using Peer Buddies With Learning Centers

Learning Center	*Activity*
Art	Invite peer buddies to make a collage together.
Blocks	Build a road from one center to the next.
Home Living	Suggest that peer buddies plan a party and set the table together.
Science	Using a magnifying glass, peer buddies can explore a rock or examine a leaf.
Math Manipulative	Ask peer buddies to count together or to count the number of objects you place on a paper plate.
Literacy	Suggest that peer buddies share their favorite books with each other.
Music	Select a song that both "buddies" like and invite them to dance to the music.
Nontraditional Center–Take Apart Center	Select unused items such as a broken cell phone or an old radio, and encourage peer buddies to explore them by taking them apart.

Classroom Activity

What I Like About You! Circle of Friendship (small group)

Cut out a large circle and divide it into pie-shaped pieces. With the circle intact, hand it to a child. Instruct the child to draw a picture of something he likes about the child next to him and then pass the circle to the next person. After everyone in the circle has drawn a picture, ask each child to describe his or her picture. On each picture, add the name of the child that the picture depicts (not the name of the artist). Later, after the class has enjoyed the picture, cut the pie-shaped wedges out and let each child take home the picture that was drawn about him and share it with his family members.

Classroom Activity

We All Have a Job to Do! (whole class)

This builds community and responsibility. Children have a new job assignment every month, so you have to assign new jobs only 9–10 times each year. You can keep track of a class list on the computer. Allow 10 minutes at the end of the day for "Job Time." Do not line up for dismissal until the room is clean and jobs are done. Remember to do some "job sharing" where two children do a big job together.

Job List:

2 mail carriers	2 lunch-line helpers
table washer	reading corner helper
plant monitor	chalkboard cleaner
supply shelf manager	library helper
center inspector	desk inspector
pencil sharpener	whiteboard cleaner
sink cleaner	math shelf help
sanitation engineer	caboose
administrative assistant	substitute (for whoever is absent)
2 scrap monsters (to pick up scraps off the floor)	

(Continued)

(Continued)

You can also do some job sharing, in which two children do a big job together.

How It Works

Jobs are posted each month on a job board. They are mounted on Velcro and attached to a board. Children select (sometimes with guided assistance) the job they want. They interview (usually only about 1 to 2 minutes). Their job responsibilities are briefly explained and then they accept the job. A letter is sent home. These can either be form letters or computer-generated letters.

Sample Letter to Family

Dear Parent of _____ (Child's name),

Your child has applied for and been hired as the scrap monster for our classroom for the month of _____. Please assist _____ (child's name) as he/she learns his/her job duties. Classroom jobs change each month. By starting early to learn how to take responsibility for keeping our "classroom community" a safe and healthy place for everyone, your child is learning to be a good citizen.

His/Her job responsibilities are as follows:

1. Help his/her coworker pick up scraps of paper on the floor.
2. Help the teacher put paper in the "recycle bin" at school.
3. Remind others to recycle or throw paper away instead of putting it on the floor.

Thank you,
(Child's teacher)

Books That Support Social Competence

Attachment

> *The Teddy Bear* by David McPhail
> *The Kissing Hand* by Audrey Shook
> *Tight Times* by Barbara Shook
> *By the Dawn's Early Light* by Karen Ackerman

Affiliation

> *Fluffy and Baron* by Marci Twain
> *We Are Best Friends* by Aliki
> *Miss Smith's Incredible Storybook* by Michael Garland

Respect for Self and Others

> *Edward the Emu* by Sheena Knowles
> *Understand and Care* by Cheri J. Meiners
> *Respect and Take Care of Things* by Cheri J. Meiners

Self-Control

> *I Ain't Gonna Paint No More* by Karen Beaumont

Problem Solving

> *Charlie Anderson* by Barbara Abercrombie
> *Talk and Work It Out* by Cheri Meiners (Free Spirit Press)

Initiative to Try New Things

> *Edwina the Emu* by Sheena Knowles
> *He Came With the Couch* by David Slonim

Acceptance of Others Who May Be Different

> *Susan Laughs* by Jeanne Willis
> *Rolling Along With Goldilocks and the Three Bears* by Cindy Meyers
> *A Day's Work* by Eve Bunting
> *Flop Ear* by Guido Van Genechten

A Sense of "Safety"

> *When I Feel Afraid* by Cheri Meiners
> *The Horrible Kirk McCruel* by Harriet Isecke

The Ability to Work in Groups and Alone

> *Join in and Play* by Cheri J. Meiners
> *The Magical Mystical Marvelous Coat* by Catherine Ann Cullen

A Healthy Sense of Self

> *Good Thing You're Not an Octopus* by Julie Markes
> *I Like Myself* by Karen Beaumont
> *I Love My Hair* by Natasha Anastashia Tarpley

Strategy

Defend Yourself With What You Say!

Purpose: The purpose of this strategy is to provide a method for all children in the classroom to use when they experience firsthand or see someone being bullied.

Focus: Tell the class that you are going to help them learn what to do about bullying. Explain that bullying is when someone is teased, pushed, hit, laughed at, or "picked on" by others. Explain that friends do not bully each other.

Develop:
1. Develop the activity by giving a few examples and asking children to raise their hands if they think the person is being bullied. Use examples that involve teasing, leaving someone out of an activity, hitting another person, laughing, and so on.
2. Explain that bullying occurs whenever children feel "left out" or unhappy because others have teased or excluded them. Explain that bullies are not "cool" and that being a bully is for someone who does not like herself very much.
3. Read a story about bullying, such as *Flop Ear* by Guido VanGretchen, and ask how the child who was being bullied might have felt. Talk about those who witnessed the bullying and ask the class how they might have prevented or stopped it from happening.

Practice:

1. Show three picture cards: one that depicts someone standing up for themselves, one that shows someone walking away, and one that shows someone going to get an adult.
2. Talk about the three choices that children have when they see or experience bullying.
3. Provide some new examples and ask the children to point to a picture card that best describes what to do.
4. Close the activity with the poem shown here, emphasizing the last two lines.
5. Make a poster of the poem and refer to it often.

Figure 12.4   From p. 93, Sprung, Froschl, and Hinitz. (2005). *The Anti-Bullying and Teasing Book.* Beltsville, MD: Gryphon House. Reprinted with permission.

Reflect:

1. Identify children who are likely targets and spend extra time reviewing this activity with them.
2. Think about whom in the class might be a "bully." Spend time talking with him about being a leader and helping others.

The Bully
By Clarissa Willis

When someone tries to bully you

Don't stand there until it's through.

Find a teacher or adult friend

They can make the teasing end.

Defend yourself with what you say

Then turn your back and walk away.

Strategy

Rainbows!

Purpose: The purpose of this strategy is to use a rainbow to demonstrate how we can work together to make something beautiful.

Focus: Show the children a picture of a rainbow. Ask them to name some of the colors they see. Explain that we are also like a rainbow because when we work together, we can make something beautiful.

Develop:
1. Hold up strips of paper in several colors (strips may be made from construction paper or ribbon). Invite each child to take a different colored strip.
2. Copy Rainbow Song on chart paper, and sing it for the children, pointing to each line as you sing.

Practice:
1. Invite the children to sing the song with you while they wave their colored paper or ribbon strips above them. Sing one line, and then ask them to repeat it after you. If a child with special needs cannot sing, invite the child to wave her paper while the class is singing.
2. Divide children into small groups and ask each group to create a rainbow with their strips of paper. Provide glue and large drawing paper for the rainbows.

Reflect:
1. Try to identify children who may need extra help participating in the activity. What might you do to help them partially participate?
2. Think about other ways that could be used to teach individual differences.

Illustration by Justin Mitchel

Rainbow Song
Adapted by Clarissa Willis
(Sung to the tune of Twinkle Twinkle Little Star)

Different colors orange and blue,

Along with other colors too!

Alone they are not much to show,

But look at them in my rainbow.

Different colors all aglow,

Making up my bright rainbow.

TERMS USED IN THIS CHAPTER

food jags—a particular food that the child eats exclusively. For example, a child will only eat peanut butter or only eat soft foods.

partial participation—a child takes part in an activity, even if he is unable to complete the task independently.

socially competent—a person who is able to manage and handle social situations easily.

SUGGESTED READING

Carol-Rich, S., Engelbrecht, J. A., Sanborn, C., Essery, E., DiMarco, N., Velez, L., & Levy, L. (2006). Growing with EASE: Eating, activity, and self-esteem. *Young Children, 61*(3), 26–30.

Laursen, E. K. (2005). Rather than fixing kids—build positive peer cultures: Reclaiming children and youth. *The Journal of Strength-based Interventions, 14*(3), 137–145.

Sprung, B., Froschl, M., & Hinitz, B. (2005). *The anti-bullying and teasing book*. Beltsville, MD: Gryphon House.

Preparing the Environment

13

Figure 13.1   Select materials that encourage motor skill development.

THE IMPORTANT ROLE OF THE ENVIRONMENT

The classroom environment plays an important role in a blended classroom. Children with special needs can be successful in a blended classroom. However, placement alone does not guarantee that this will happen. In other words, just being in the presence of their peers does not automatically guarantee a child with special needs will learn from them. In order for success to occur, several components must be in place: (a) a delicate balance between teacher-directed and child-directed activities within the context of a daily routine; (b) materials and learning centers that are adapted for children with special needs; (c) carefully planned intentional instruction; and (d) adequate support systems for the child (Brown, Hemmeter, & Pretti-Frontczak, 2005).

In order to plan developmentally appropriate experiences for a child with special needs, it is critical that adequate support systems are already in place before the child is enrolled. For example, what support services will the child receive (speech therapy, occupational therapy, etc.) and when will those support services take place? In addition, it is critical to know if the child will have a one-on-one assistant or if there will be a teacher assistant assigned to several children. The teacher should also know if the child already uses any assistive technology devices, such as a machine to talk or adaptive switches to turn on battery-operated toys. Most important, the teacher must know how the child communicates with others (talk, sign language, gestures) and if the child has any specific behavioral characteristics that will interfere with his participation in routine classroom activities (loud outbursts, fear of water, self-stimulation such as hand wringing or hand flapping).

Imagine how Dionne, a five-year-old child with cerebral palsy, might feel if he arrives in your classroom and spots a sparkling crystal rock in the science/nature center. Eagerly, he goes over to the center for a closer look, only to discover that the magnifying glasses you have for students to use are not adapted so that a child with limited motor skills can use them. Instead of actively exploring his newfound treasure, he is relegated to watching others do it. The materials in the room, the learning centers, and the activities planned should be adapted in such a way that a child with special needs can be an active participant. In order for this to occur, the teacher and her assistant must know as much as possible about the child before the first day of school (see Chapter 11 for more about gathering information from families).

Most early childhood settings are structured so that children have multiple opportunities to make choices and explore various learning centers. By the time they reach preschool and kindergarten, typically developing children know how to explore new environments and can generally remain actively engaged in developmentally appropriate games and activities. Active engagement is generally defined as the time children spend interacting in an activity that is developmentally appropriate for their age and stage of development. The same is not necessarily true for children with special needs. For these children to be actively engaged, it is necessary that the teacher intentionally structure the learning environment and the activities within that environment in such a way that children with special needs learn how to become active participants. Methods that teachers can use to help children become and stay actively engaged are included in Table 13.1.

Table 13.1 Methods to Help Promote Engagement

Method	*Example*
Focus on what you want the child to know	Know, before you initiate an activity, what your goal or objective for that particular activity will be. For example, in a writing activity, your goal for most of the children in your class may be to recognize the first letter in their names and write their names on a page in their journal. Your goal for the child with special needs may be to identify the first letter in her name and trace it on a picture she has drawn in her journal.
Develop	As previously mentioned, your ultimate goal for the child with special needs will be to recognize all the letters in his name. You should look for opportunities throughout the day for the child to see the first letter of his name and cue him accordingly. For example, you may say, "Look Tony, there is the letter T." You could then hand Tony a plastic letter "T" and ask him to trace it with his fingers.
Model	Model exactly what you want the child to do. Show her each step and then ask her to do it with you. For extra practice, invite the child to show you the step you just modeled.
Prompts (visual and auditory)	Prompts are cues that you give the child that help him know what to do next. For example, if you want him to remember that the next step in an activity is to stand up, you might use a gesture to remind him.
Reflect	Allow yourself time to reflect on the activity. Think about what worked and what did not. Look for ways to take what worked and adapt it for other routines or activities.

MAINTAINING A BALANCE BETWEEN ACTIVITIES

Maintaining a balance between teacher-directed and child-initiated activities is never easy. However, one of the best resources for accomplishing this goal is the daily schedule. As a teacher, you may not have full control over your daily schedule, but it is still possible for you to design a schedule that is beneficial for all of the children in your class. When designing the schedule, keep in mind

- the types of children with special needs in your classroom;
- the attention spans of the children in your classroom;
- the essentials (center time, large group, small group, free exploration); and

- the importance of implementing a schedule that minimizes transitions.

It is also important to pay close attention to the amount of time that is spent in each activity. According to Pretti-Frontczak and Bricker (2004), a significant amount of time during the day should be spent in activities that enable teachers to be available to support children's engagement. In addition, children benefit from making choices about what they do and from opportunities to explore developmentally appropriate materials that are challenging. By examining the components of a daily schedule, we can see how to achieve this balance and how to plan activities that maximize participation by children with special needs.

THE DAILY SCHEDULE

While the kindergarten schedule is usually more academic in nature than a preschool schedule, most daily schedules will include

- large group time (usually two or more per day);
- small group time (in kindergarten this may be more structured);
- individual instruction (in kindergarten this may be more directed toward acquisition of academic skills, such as reading, math, or writing);
- free choice time (usually spent in learning centers);
- creative activities (art, music, drama);
- transitions between activities; and
- out-of-class activities (computer lab, library time, etc.).

Let's look at each of these and how they can be adapted for children with special needs.

LARGE GROUP TIME

Whether it is called circle time or large group time, this is the time during the day when the entire class is involved in a single activity. It is also the most challenging time for children with special needs (Isbell & Isbell, 2005). This is especially true for children with autism, behavior challenges, and those with extremely short attention spans. In order to make this time meaningful for children with special needs, please remember the following:

- Provide children with clear expectations for their behavior. Make sure they know what they are expected to do. Keep the expectations appropriate to their level of development and do not forget to praise them when they meet those expectations.

- Keep large group time as short as possible. For children with significant issues sitting through a whole large group activity, consider allowing them to work up to a full activity. Start by asking them to participate for a few minutes and gradually build up more time.

- Make the activity as meaningful as possible for children with special needs. This may involve giving them props to use in the activity, such as puppets, or it may involve having a different goal for them than what you have for the rest of the class.

- Modify materials and activities so the children can, at least, have partial participation. If you are teaching a difficult or complex task, break down the task into smaller steps and require the children with special needs to do part of the activity. For example, if the class is counting to 20 or to 100 by 10s, invite children with special needs to count to 10. Provide math manipulatives like "teddy bear" counters or poker chips to help them.

- Research has shown that calendar activities have little meaning for preschool-aged children. Instead talk about the weather or what the class will do on a specific day of the week.

SMALL GROUP TIME

Small group time usually involves working with a few children. If possible, keep the group size to four, especially if children with special needs are in the group. It is during small group time that more individualized and detailed instruction takes place. Select groups based on temperament as well as ability level. Some guidelines for helping children with special needs function in a small group include the following:

- Review what was previously learned.
- Remember that children with special needs have trouble generalizing information, so provide as many concrete examples as possible.
- During small group time, provide multiple opportunities for participation. Ask questions frequently and look for ways to keep the children engaged.
- Offer children opportunities to practice.
- Remember that children with special needs also need extra time to process new information.

● Provide positive feedback and do not forget to praise children for their attempts, even if those attempts are not successful.

INDIVIDUALIZED INSTRUCTION

Individualized instruction time involves the teacher or another adult working one-on-one with a child. This instruction should always be intentional and meaningful for the child. For a child with special needs, it is designed around the specific goals in her Individual Education Plan (IEP). Two methods of individualized instruction are especially effective for children with special needs. These methods are differentiated instruction and response to intervention (RTI). They will be discussed in more detail in Chapter 14 (Curriculum).

FREE CHOICE TIME

Free choice time is the child-initiated portion of the day. It is the time when children have a choice about what they do and where they do it. In an early childhood classroom, free choice time is usually spent in learning centers. Table 13.2 offers some suggestions for making modifications to traditional and a few nontraditional learning centers.

Table 13.2 Modifications for Learning Centers

Center	*Modifications*
Literacy Center	Place books, which feature people with disabilities as part of the community as well as people from other cultures, throughout the center. Attach paperclips to pages of books to serve as "page-turners" for children with fine motor skill issues. Provide page magnification for those who might need it and add a few books that have a lot of pictures and very little print.
Writing Center	Provide special pencil grips for children who cannot hold a pencil without help. Provide easels or a slanted writing board that can be adjusted to varying heights for children with vision or perception problems. Make sure lighting is adequate and does not create a glare on the paper. Provide alternatives such as magnetic letters to trace or letter cutouts to use as guides.

Math Manipulative Center	Offer math aids such as counters. Make sure materials vary in size, color, and texture. Make geometric shapes such as circles, squares and triangles.
Science Center	Offer magnifying glasses of varying strengths. If possible, try to provide a magnifying glass with a built-in light. Provide large and small items to explore. Add a pair of tongs to help children with fine motor issues pick up objects. Make sure some activities involve measuring both liquids and solids, as this reinforces math skills.
Geography Center	Provide maps of varying textures and sizes. Encourage children to identify their state by its shape.
Block Center	Provide blocks of all sizes and shapes. Use blocks to help reinforce concepts of opposite pairs, such as big/little, over/under, up/down, and in/out.
Art Center	Provide adaptive paintbrushes for children with motor issues. Make sure art materials are available in bright colors. Provide a variety of textures and art mediums (clay, paint, paper, sand, etc.) to encourage exploration of new things.
Computer Center	Make sure there is an adaptive keyboard, such as Intellikeys™, which provides adaptive keyboard overlays for children with special needs. Provide computer programs for varying abilities and skills. Programs that offer instant feedback are especially good for children with special needs.
Quiet Center	Include comfortable seating such as a beanbag chair or soft pillows and instead of overhead lighting create soft lighting with lamps. Provide an audio player with headphones so children can listen to music. If necessary, fit the player with an adaptive switch or battery interrupter so children can turn it on and off.
Dress-Up Center	Place clothes with buttons and zippers in the dress-up center. This will give children extra practice. Provide clothes of varying colors and invite children to sort them by color, shape, size, and so on.
Home Living Center	Make sure some of the materials have large handles for the child to grip. Home living is a great center to role-play activities such as enjoying meals with friends and routines such as getting ready for bed or getting ready for school. Place sequence cards for everyday things like setting the table or getting ready for school in the center. The cards will help children learn the steps of routine activities.

(Continued)

Table 13.2   (Continued)

Nontraditional Centers	
Tactile Center	Provide materials and items of varying shapes, textures, and sizes. Make "feely" boxes with things of different textures hidden inside. Remember, some children may be hesitant to put their hands into a box. Offer to do the activity with these children.
Healthy Living Center	Activities might include a unit on how to keep from catching a cold or choices of healthy foods to eat.
Friendship Center	This center can reinforce in-class activities by giving children an opportunity to practice friendship skills. Sequence cards, role-playing activities, or friendship circles (a circle where friends sit and talk) are all useful activities that help children with special needs interact with their peers.
International Center	Feature people and places that are different. Provide props to go with each activity. This center can enable you to continue to teach about diversity. Bring foods from other cultures to sample as well. This helps children learn about new and different tastes. This is a good center for collaborative activities.

TRANSITIONS

Transitions between activities can be especially problematic for children with special needs. The following are a few strategies that teachers can use to make transitions go more smoothly.

1. Let the child know before it is time to transition. This can be accomplished by showing her a timer, giving her a specified cue, such as a tap on the shoulder, or simply telling her that it is almost time to transition.
2. Make transitions fun. Invite the children to fly like airplanes or birds, walk like an elephant (arms can swing in front for the trunk), gallop like a pony, or tiptoe like a mouse.
3. Use transition helpers, such as music or sound. A song played or sung at each transition can be a great cue that it is time to transition. A xylophone, chime, or a small tinkling bell can also help. Avoid loud noises, such as a large bell or gong, as these are especially annoying for children with sensory integration issues.

ASSISTIVE TECHNOLOGY—ADAPTING MATERIALS

Today's technology is making it possible for children with disabilities to do more for themselves than ever thought possible. A child who cannot use his hands can operate a computer with a switch or an on-screen keyboard. A child with speech problems can communicate using a portable electronic device that "speaks." Assistive technology can mean anything from simple, homemade devices to highly sophisticated environmental control systems. Assistive technology includes adapted toys with battery interrupter switches, computers with special screens or keyboards, wheelchairs powered by a simple toggle switch, or augmentative communication devices that speak for nonverbal children. In other words, assistive technology takes in a wide range of items from special switches to commercially available computers that assist an individual with learning, working, and interacting socially. In summary, assistive technology devices are mechanical aids, which substitute for or enhance the function of some physical or mental ability that is impaired.

Assistive technology includes a broad range of devices from "low tech" (e.g., pencil grips, splints, easels, etc.) to "high tech" (e.g., computers, voice synthesizers, Braille readers, etc.). The Individuals with Disabilities Education Act (IDEA), the federal special education law, provides this legal definition of an assistive technology device: "any item, piece of equipment, or product system . . . that is used to increase, maintain, or improve functional capabilities of individuals with disabilities." Under IDEA, assistive technology devices can be used in the educational setting to provide a variety of accommodations or adaptations for

Figure 13.2 Adapt materials to meet the goals for children with special needs.

people with disabilities. IDEA lists the services a school district may need to provide in order to ensure that assistive technology is useful to a child at school. In addition to an assistive technology evaluation of the technology needs of the child, IDEA also says that schools should

- purchase, lease, or otherwise provide for the acquisition of assistive technology devices for individuals with disabilities;
- select, design, fit, customize, adapt, apply, maintain, repair, or replace assistive technology devices;
- coordinate and use other therapies, interventions, or services with assistive technology devices, such as those associated with existing education and rehabilitation plans and programs;
- provide assistive technology training or technical assistance with assistive technology for an individual with a disability, or, where appropriate, the family of an individual with disabilities; and
- provide training or technical assistance for professionals, employers, or other individuals who provide services to, employ, or otherwise are substantially involved in the major life functions of individuals with disabilities.

One note of caution, however, is that most young children are not developmentally ready for expensive complicated technology. For young children, it is usually better to start out with low-tech devices and work up to products that are more sophisticated. A complete listing of assistive technology products and where they can be purchased can be found in the Appendix.

SUMMARY

Remember, the environment can be structured in such a way that all children learn. In order to do that, teachers must strike a balance between teacher-directed and child-centered activities, adapt and accommodate activities for children with special needs, and differentiate instruction in such a way that children who are able can master content standards.

Now that we know how to structure the environment so that it is fun, exciting, and rewarding for all students, especially students with special needs, let's look at some strategies we can use to make everyday routines and activities more exciting and challenging.

Strategy

Starting off Right—A Morning Greeting

Purpose: The purpose of this strategy is to help everyone feel welcome in a small group setting and to help children learn each other's names.

Focus: Tell the class that you are going to teach them a welcome song. Explain that you will be singing the song to help them learn the names of all their friends at school.

Develop:

1. Develop the activity by reciting the welcome chant to the children.
2. Ask each child to wave back at the others in the circle when she hears her name used in the chant.
3. Demonstrate how to wave. For children with special needs who do not know how to wave, model it again for them.

Practice:

1. Recite the chant once and see if the child in the chant waves her hand.
2. Remind the group that they are supposed to wave when the words of the chant say wave.
3. Continue to recite the chant until each child in the group has had a turn.

Reflect:

1. Identify children who were hesitant to participate. Think of ways to encourage them to interact with others.
2. Think about other ways that the activity may need to be adapted for children with special needs.

Welcome Chant

Welcome, _____ (child's name),

Welcome _____.

Your friends will wave at you!

(Children in group wave at child whose name was used)

(Encourage child to wave back at the group)

They are glad you're here today, and I am happy, too!

Strategy

All About Me! Book

Purpose: The purpose of this strategy is to encourage association in the classroom community and help children tell each other about themselves.

Focus: Tell the children that they are going to make an "All About Me! Book" to share with the class. Show them a book that you have made about yourself. Keep it simple, with a few pages and perhaps some pictures of you with a pet or on a family vacation.

Develop:
1. Fold four sheets of white paper in half and put a staple in the middle to make a book. Make the cover out of construction paper.
2. Ask each child to write a sentence on each page about himself or something he likes to do with family members or friends. For younger children, invite them to dictate the sentence to you.
3. For children with vision or motor issues, make their book larger, so it will be easier for them to use. If the child is unable to draw a picture, ask him to cut out a picture or bring a picture from home for his book. For children who may not have access to pictures from home, use a digital camera to take a few shots of the child doing something at school.
4. Invite the children to share their books. It may take several days to write, illustrate, and complete each book. This activity could be stretched across multiple days with a few children "reading" their book to the group each day.

Practice:
1. This activity provides an opportunity to practice what children have already learned about books (e.g., they have a title, an author, a beginning, a middle, and an end).
2. Talk to the class about fiction (stories that are not real) and nonfiction (stories that are real).

3. To expand and build new knowledge, talk about the words biography (a true story written about someone by another person) and autobiography (a true story written about you by you). This activity can be easily tailored to meet the needs of diverse learners who have varying levels of literacy skills.

4. For additional practice, put an audio recorder in the quiet center or another learning center in the room and ask children to record sentences about themselves.

Reflect:

1. Identify ways to adapt this activity for a child who is nonverbal. For example, you could ask her family to write sentences about her, get someone to record the sentences, and play the recording for the class.

2. If some children seem too shy and withdrawn to share their books, think of ways to get them to participate, such as reading the book to you without other children present or reading the book with one friend in the quiet center.

Strategy

Getting to Know You (Meeting the Workers at My School)

Purpose: The purpose of this strategy is to help students with special needs learn about the people who work at their school.

Focus: Tell the children that they will be learning about the people who work at the school. If possible, make picture cards with photographs of the workers at the school, such as the bus driver, cafeteria worker, office staff, principal, librarian, and so on.

Develop:

1. If possible, during the first few weeks of school, invite different workers to come to the class, introduce themselves, and talk about what they do.

2. After each worker has spoken, take the child (or a small group of children) to visit him for a few minutes in his place of work.

Practice:

1. Make a bulletin board in the classroom that depicts the workers at the school doing their jobs.
2. Play a game with a small group of children. Say, "I am thinking about the lady who serves our meals in the cafeteria. Her name is _____." If no one responds, provide a prompt, such as asking, "Could someone go to the bulletin board and point to her picture for me?"
3. Throughout the course of the day, as you and the class pass various areas at school, such as the library, cafeteria, and principal's office, ask questions about who works in each place.

Reflect:

1. Children with more significant special needs may be unable to name all the workers; decide on one or two that are most important and try to help the child learn who they are. In addition, if the child cannot verbalize the name of the person, try to see if he can point to that person's picture using the picture cards you made.

Strategy

I Spy! Making Discoveries in My Classroom

Purpose: The purpose of this strategy is to help students with special needs learn about items from various locations in the classroom.

Focus: This strategy works well in a small group of children. Bring a large basket from home and go around the room gathering items from different locations. Include such things as a magnifying glass, writing implement, something from the art area, a book from the library center, and an item from home living. Tell the children that you will be talking to them about the items in your basket.

Develop:

1. Hold up the first item and describe it for the children. Ask a volunteer to tell you where the item came from. You may need to offer some extra clues to help the students identify the item.

When you finish, hand the item to one child and ask her to place it back in the center or area where it belongs.

2. Continue with all the items in your basket or until every child has had a turn at identifying the item in the basket and returning it to its "home."

Practice:

1. After you finish the activity, take a walk around the classroom and try to identify the items from your basket.
2. To build vocabulary skills, see if you can get students to name other items that they see in each center.
3. Ask students to show you items that they cannot name. Name the "new" item for the children and ask them to say the name after you. Remember that children with sensory impairments may need to explore items in a different way, such as touching them or learning the name of the object in sign language.

Reflect:

1. Children with more significant special needs may be unable to name all the items. Select one or two that are most important and try to help the child learn to identify them. Remember to select items that are functional for the child.
2. If a child is having difficulty learning the names of some of the main items in each center, make a set of picture cards and send them home with her. Invite her family to help her practice identifying the items on the cards. Keep in mind that many children with special needs relate better to real pictures than abstract drawings.

TERMS USED IN THIS CHAPTER

active engagement—generally defined as the time children spend interacting in an activity that is developmentally appropriate for their age and stage of development.

assistive technology—technology, whether low- or high-tech, that assists a person in doing an activity or life skill that he would be unable to perform without such help.

augmentative communication—a device that serves as a person's primary mode of communication and speaks for her. It usually involves a series of prerecorded responses using either live voice or digital technology.

partial participation—when a child with special needs participates in an activity as much as possible, even if he cannot fully complete the activity in the same manner as his peers.

prompts—a cue or clue that is used to help a child with special needs know what she needs to do. Sometimes prompts are physical, such as a tap on the shoulder, and other times they include the use of a keyword or phrase.

temperament—the way a child behaves or reacts that is characteristic of that child.

RESOURCES USED IN THIS CHAPTER

Brown, J. G., Hemmeter, M. L., & Pretti-Frontczak, K. (2005). *Blended practices for teaching young children in inclusive settings.* Baltimore, MD: Paul H. Brookes.

Isbell, C., & Isbell, R. (2005). *The inclusive learning center book for preschool children with special needs.* Beltsville, MD: Gryphon House Publishing.

Pretti-Frontczak, K., & Bricker, D. (2004). *An activity based approach to early intervention* (3rd ed.). Baltimore, MD: Paul H. Brookes Publishing Company.

SUGGESTED READING

Cook, R. J. (2004). Embedding assessment of young children into routines of inclusive settings: A systematic planning approach. *Young Exceptional Children, 7*(3), 2–11.

Isbell, R., & Exelby, B. (2001). *Early learning environments that work!* Beltsville, MD: Gryphon House.

Nikolaraizi, M., Kumar, P., Favazza, P., Sideridis, G., Koulousiou, D., & Riall, A. (2005). A cross-cultural examination of typically developing children's attitudes toward individuals with special needs. *International Journal of Disability Development and Education, 52*(2), 101–119. (ERIC Document Reproduction Service No. EJ691257)

Noonan, M. J., & McCormick, L. (2006). *Young children with disabilities in natural environments: Methods and procedures.* Baltimore, MD: Paul H. Brookes.

The Curriculum 14

Figure 14.1   The curriculum should allow for one-on-one instruction.

WHAT ROLE DOES THE CURRICULUM PLAY IN TEACHING CHILDREN WITH SPECIAL NEEDS?

For the purposes of this book, curriculum is defined as both the content and composition of classroom instruction. This includes all daily activities, such as transitions, routines, schedules, and content area instruction, which impact children's physical, social, emotional, and intellectual development. In order to meet the unique learning needs of children with special needs, the following must occur:

- Authentic assessments conducted in natural environments
- Targeting functional skills and behaviors based on those assessments

- Designing and implementing individualized instruction
- Monitoring the child to determine her progress

IS THERE A SPECIAL "CURRICULUM" FOR A CHILD WITH SPECIAL NEEDS?

Certainly, there are commercial curriculums that are written specifically for children with special needs. However, because instruction for children with special needs must be individualized, there is not one "perfect" curriculum that will be appropriate for every child. More important than finding a specific curriculum is knowing what elements must be incorporated into any activity planned for an inclusive early childhood setting. Regardless of the curriculum selected, it is essential that the curriculum is designed to take into account

- scientifically-based research about how young children learn;
- outcomes that meet national, state, and local standards and guidelines; and
- outcomes recommended by national organizations (e.g., National Association for the Education of Young Children, Council for Exceptional Children, International Reading Association, etc.).

CURRICULUM MODELS

The term curriculum model refers to an educational system that combines theory with practice. A curriculum model is generally based on a theory and knowledge base that reflects a philosophical orientation. Scientifically based research and educational evaluation should be the foundation of any curriculum model. While many commercial companies have developed curriculum models that are sound and support child development, curriculum models will be discussed here only in the broadest sense of the type of curriculum models that are on the market. The basic components of a sound curriculum model include

- physical environment guidelines;
- suggestions for structuring activities;
- components that discuss interacting with children and their families; and
- content area instruction that is developmentally appropriate.

Two models of instruction that have direct implications for children with special needs are differentiated instruction and response to intervention (RTI).

DIFFERENTIATED INSTRUCTION (DI)

Differentiated instruction is based on the premise that because students vary in their ability levels, interests, and learning needs, there should be multiple ways in which those needs are met. Central to the concept of differentiated instruction are the following beliefs:

- Students differ in their learning styles; each student has individual strengths and weaknesses.
- Classrooms in which students are active learners, decision makers, and problem solvers are more natural and effective than those in which students are served a "one-size-fits-all" curriculum and are treated as passive recipients of information.
- Making meaning out of important ideas is more important than just "covering topics" about subjects.

The key to a differentiated classroom is that all students are regularly offered choices. This concept of choice making is especially applicable to children with special needs. Proponents of differentiated instruction feel that the curriculum should be differentiated in three main ways: (a) children need multiple options for receiving information, (b) children need varying ways to process the information they receive, and (c) children need more than one way to express what they have learned.

Embedded in differentiated instruction is a concept known as universal design for learning applications, or UDL. According to Hall, Stragman, and Meyer (2003),

> UDL calls for the design of curricula with the needs of all students in mind, so that methods, materials, and assessment are usable by all. Traditional curricula present a host of barriers that limit students' access to information and learning. Of these, printed text is particularly notorious. In a traditional curriculum, a student without a well-developed ability to see, decode, attend to, or comprehend printed text is compelled to adapt to its ubiquity as best as he or she can. In contrast, a UDL curriculum is designed to be innately flexible, enriched with multiple media so that alternatives can be accessed whenever appropriate. A UDL curriculum takes on the burden of adaptation so that the student doesn't have to, minimizing barriers and maximizing access to both information and learning. (An Introduction to Universal Design for Learning Applications section, ¶ 2)

RESPONSE TO INTERVENTION (RTI)

Response to intervention is a promising approach to help identify students who are at risk for learning disabilities and to work with all students to ensure their educational success. While RTI was first designed to help school-aged children who were struggling with content area subject matter, it can, on some levels, be applied to younger children as well. RTI is based on the idea that, if data on how children are performing across specific areas of learning and behavior are examined, and intervention with well-planned intentional instruction occurs before they start to fail, then we can, in essence, intervene before they reach the point of academic failure. In other words, the idea behind RTI is that by starting at the earliest possible moment when a child is at risk for learning disabilities, that risk can be greatly reduced. RTI is the basis for a model that has emerged recently called recognition and response.

RECOGNITION AND RESPONSE

The intent behind recognition and response is not to "label" children early and send them to special education classes. Rather, it is based on the idea that, by intervening early, we may be able to prevent some children from needing special education services. The basic components of recognition and response include the following:

- Recognizing a child's strengths and early signs of difficulties with learning may help that child succeed rather than fail academically.
- Responding with appropriate activities and learning experiences will give the child a better chance at success.
- Providing information to a child's family and future teachers is an important step toward helping that child in the future.

Learning disabilities are rarely evident in young children and usually are not diagnosed until the child is in the second or third grade. Recognition and response and RTI do not propose to identify and diagnose learning disabilities in young children. Instead, they are models of instruction designed to help those students before they are referred for special education testing. In summary, RTI and recognition and response hope to make a connection between early care and early school settings so that information about children and effective teaching practices can be shared between settings and among parents and professionals.

Research into both models is ongoing in institutions such as the Frank Porter Graham Institute at Chapel Hill, North Carolina, and the IRIS Center at Vanderbilt in Nashville, Tennessee, as they gather data and conduct scientifically based research to help determine the relationship and applicability between RTI and early childhood settings. Certainly, in the coming months and years, more information about how these models apply to children in preschool and kindergarten will become available.

Regardless of the model selected, it is important to know how to accommodate the unique learning needs of all children and how to make modifications to the curriculum that maximize a child's individual strengths.

CURRICULUM MODIFICATIONS FOR CHILDREN WITH SPECIAL NEEDS

Modifications to the curriculum fall into several broad categories, as shown in Table 14.1:

Table 14.1   Curriculum Modifications

Modification	*Example*
Adaptations to the learning environment	Making classroom aisles wider, so that learning centers are accessible to a child in a wheelchair Placing sequence cards in each center to help the child with cognitive challenges know what to do
Special equipment or assistive technology adaptations	A special computer keyboard that is accessible to a child with severe motor impairments Adaptive equipment, such as a walker or prone stander
Modifications of the lesson or activity content	Modifying a math activity by allowing the child with special needs to use manipulatives to help him count
Modifications or adaptations in expectations for the learner	Children may be asked to write their names, while the child with special needs traces her name or writes the first letter of her name.
Adult support	In some cases, an assistant may be assigned to a child on a one-on-one basis to help with his personal needs such as going to the bathroom or eating

Figure 14.2   Picture schedules help children with special needs understand what to do next.

CONTENT AREA INSTRUCTION

Literacy

Literacy means much more than just learning how to read. Literacy encompasses knowledge of how to read, write, and use language in meaningful ways. High-quality, early childhood education programs have great potential for preventing later school failure, particularly if they place a strong emphasis on language development (Bernhard, Winsler, Bleiker, Ginieniewicz, & Madigan, 2005; Juel, 2006). For this reason, early childhood teachers need comprehensive knowledge about language and about how to help children develop language and literacy skills. In order to effectively implement literacy activities in the preschool and kindergarten classroom, teachers should know how to conduct story reading and other early literacy experiences that promote phonological awareness and prepare children for later success in reading (Snow, Burns, & Griffin, 1998). In addition, early childhood teachers should develop an understanding of (a) cultural and linguistic diversity, (b) the challenges that children with special needs encounter, and (c) strategies that recognize that many children do not have opportunities for language-learning activities at home (Mooney, 2005).

Fisch, Smith, and Phinney (1997) found that children from at-risk environments, who were given extensive exposure to rich language and interactive experiences and who were read to from birth and in the preschool environment, showed increases in IQ of 15 to 30 points over children from similar environments who were not given this stimulation. The earlier the stimulation began, the greater the results. Intervention that did not begin until kindergarten had a minuscule impact by comparison (Dickinson & Tabors, 2001).

Since the release of the report from the National Literacy Panel in the late 1990s, there has been an ongoing discussion about what constitutes appropriate early literacy instruction. According to the Committee on the Prevention of Reading Difficulties in Young Children, "Of the many conditions that appear to contribute to successful reading by school children, among the more important are each child's (1) intellectual and sensory capacities; (2) positive expectations about and experiences with literacy from an early age; (3) support for reading-related activities and attitudes so that he or she is prepared to benefit from early literacy experiences and subsequent formal instruction in school; and (4) instructional environments conducive to learning" (Snow, Burns, & Griffin, 1998).

The committee concluded that, in order for initial reading instruction to be effective and to produce long-term positive outcomes, it must require that children be able to

1. use reading to obtain meaning from print;
2. have multiple opportunities to read;
3. understand sound-spelling relationships;
4. learn about the nature of the alphabetic writing system; and
5. understand how spoken words are structured.

Although researchers continue to debate what constitutes quality early literacy instruction, most experts agree the research indicates that quality programs address the following: listening skills, phonological awareness, fluency, vocabulary, and comprehension. Suggestions for helping to develop literacy skills in children with special needs include the following:

- Rhymes and finger plays that encourage children to use rhyming words
- Games that associate letters with the sounds they make, as well as physical representations of letters (letters made from different materials or different textures)
- Stories read often with opportunities for the child to ask questions and explore aspects of the story like sequencing the events in the story
- Reading stories with visual cues such as props, puppets, and objects
- Opportunities and practice in using words in sentences and in context
- Learning about environmental print (bathroom signs, stop, exit, etc.)
- Opportunities to practice early literacy skills at home

While children with special needs are in and of themselves more likely than their typically developing peers to have difficulties with reading, the following are some of the red flags identified as indicators that a preschool child may be at risk for having significant challenges learning to read.

Writing

Writing certainly can be considered an important functional or life-long skill for everyone. While formal instruction in writing is not developmentally appropriate in a preschool setting, there are certainly some "prewriting" skills that can and should be taught. Since many children with special needs will have lifelong difficulties producing written words that are legible, it is important that their early writing experiences be as rewarding as possible. Based on the individual needs of each child, it may be necessary to provide adaptive materials, such as large pencils, specialized pencil grips, or adaptive handles.

In cases where the child has significant motor delays, an adaptive keyboard may be his primary means of producing written words. Opportunities should be offered that help children with special needs learn to write words and phrases that are functional, such as their name, address, and so on. According to Isbell and Isbell (2005), a child with special needs will need to learn these skills in regard to prewriting: (a) proper posture needed for writing; (b) practice imitating simple shapes or letters using a finger or writing instrument; (c) ability to use a functional grasp of a writing utensil; and (d) ability to trace simple shapes or letters using a finger or writing utensil. Depending on the extent of the child's motor impairments, it may also be necessary to provide an easel that can be tilted or an elevated writing surface.

Math

Math instruction in an early childhood setting usually involves counting, measuring, and dealing with general number concepts. Although diagnosing math related learning disabilities usually occurs later, when the child is older, there are some early warning signs that have been identified by the National Center for Learning Disabilities. These early warning signs include

1. crying or getting angry when working with numbers;
2. difficulty remembering numbers;
3. having trouble identifying shapes, even after much repetition;
4. inability to distinguish left from right; and
5. being extremely restless and failing to sit still.

Suggestions for teaching number skills to children with special needs include the following:

1. Because children with special needs require extra practice, look for opportunities throughout the day to count things. Count the number of children in each learning center, the number of children wearing blue shirts, the plates for snack, the number of crayons in the art area, and so on.
2. Provide help when asking children to count. Use paper plates as placeholders and ask children to count the items on a plate.
3. Remember to use and practice words related to number concepts such as large/small, few/many, and so on.

4. Encourage children to measure things using a measuring tape. Talk about measurement in terms of bigger than or more than.
5. Provide opportunities to pick out shapes around the classroom. Draw a shape on the floor and invite children to walk it off with you. Describe the shape as round or square.

Strategy

Creating a Literacy-Rich Environment

Purpose: The purpose of this strategy is to help teachers prepare a literacy-rich environment that is beneficial for children with special needs.

Focus: Think about the types of children with special needs in your classroom and consider how you might adapt literacy activities to meet their needs.

Develop: Create a literacy-rich environment by adding the following to your literacy area or literacy learning center:

1. Word/letter games like Pictionary, Scrabble, BINGO, and Boggle
2. Alphabet letter cookie cutters or stamps
3. Environment print
4. Magnetic letters and cookie sheets
5. Labeled photos of students, teachers, important school staff, and class activities
6. Books, magazines, recorded books, books on computer
7. Labeled items in your classroom

Practice:
1. Give children with special needs the opportunity to practice telling and retelling stories to each other using picture sequence cards, if necessary.
2. Plan activities that help children identify survival words in their environment, such as open/close, on/off, exit, bathroom, poison, and emergency.
3. For children with special needs, make it a priority that they learn to write their name and home address as well as at least one phone number where a parent can be reached.

Reflect:
1. Children with special needs will require extra practice, so think about ways you can incorporate literacy into your daily routines.
2. Children with special needs are more prone to want to learn about things that interest them, so try to provide books about those subjects.

Strategy

Helping Children With Special Needs Develop Math Skills

Purpose: The purpose of this strategy is to provide suggestions for teachers that help them recognize and plan activities to teach essential math skills to children with special needs.

Focus: Think about the types of children with special needs in your classroom and consider how you could adapt math activities to meet their needs. Look at the essential math skills they will need throughout their lives such as counting, measuring, and using money.

Develop: Incorporate the following into your math learning center or math activities.

Make Numbers: It is important to have numbers and number words around so children can see them. Here are some simple "Number Ideas" activities:

1. Make numbers out of pipe cleaners.
2. Use magnetic numbers and encourage children to count out items to match each number.
3. Make number sculptures out of clay or play-dough.
4. Take a paper plate and write a number on it, or cut out a number and paste it

Figure 14.3   Drawing of paper plate numbers.
Illustration by Justin Mitchel

on the plate. Invite a child to count out objects to match that number. This is especially effective for children with visual impairments as it gives them a surface to count on.

Measurement: Encourage measurement by providing a measuring tape and modeling how to use it. Incorporate words that imply measurement into daily activities such as tallest, shortest, longest, first, second, and so on.

Practice:
1. Give children with special needs the opportunity to practice counting items and objects within the classroom.
2. Plan activities that help children identify number concepts such as first, last, next.
3. For children with special needs, make it a priority that they learn to count and use real money, as this is a functional life skill that is crucial for independence.

Reflect:
1. Children with special needs will require extra practice, so think about ways you can incorporate practicing new number skills.
2. Children with special needs are more prone to want to learn about things that interest them, so try to provide books about those subjects and use the books to help the child understand number concepts. For example, read a book about a dinosaur then count the dinosaurs in the book.

Strategy

Planning Science Activities for Children With Special Needs

Purpose: The purpose of this strategy is to help teachers prepare science activities for children with special needs.

Focus: Science is not just a collection of facts. It includes

- observing what's happening;
- predicting what might happen;
- testing predictions under controlled conditions to see if they are correct; and
- trying to make sense of our observations.

Figure 14.4   Science includes testing predictions about sound.

Develop:

1. Children with special needs learn science best if they have a hands-on approach.
2. Hands-on science can also help children think critically and gain confidence in their own ability to solve problems.
3. What engages very young children? Things they can see, touch, manipulate, and modify or situations that allow them to figure out what happens—in short, events and puzzles they can investigate, which is the very stuff of science.

Practice:

1. Classifying activities: Gather a collection of items to be classified, such as leaves, shoes, empty food containers, or items of clothing. Be sure to add one or two things that do not belong in the collection.
2. Invite children to classify items with a friend. For children with special needs, it will be easier if they have a container such as a bucket or narrow tube to put the items in as they classify them. Provide tongs to help children with items that may be difficult to pick up.

Reflect:

1. Think about ways to adapt equipment in your science center. Place a sponge hair roller on the handle of the magnifying glass

to provide an easier surface for the child to grip or provide a stationary magnifying device for children who have motor skills issues.

2. Look for ways to help children with special needs record what they see. If they are unable to record data or produce a graph, invite a friend to serve as the "administrative assistant" and help them.

Strategy

Teaching Children With Special Needs About Personal Safety

Purpose: The purpose of this strategy is to help teachers instruct children with special needs about personal safety.

Focus: Teaching children about personal safety is especially important for children with special needs, as they are at higher risk than their peers for being targeted by sexual predators.

Develop: Help children learn about "Stranger Danger" in the following ways:

1. Make a poster about the "Stranger Rules."
2. Emphasize the following: children should never get in the car with someone they do not know; children should not take food or drink from someone they do not know; if someone says their parents (sisters, pets, etc.) are hurt, they are not to believe them, unless they know them well. Children should never pet an animal that belongs to a stranger. Adults do not need directions, help, or information from children.
3. Talk about the importance of staying with a group and not going off alone.

Practice:

1. Practice the personal safety rules and play games where you make up a scenario and ask children what to do.
2. Make sure all children know their names, addresses, contact phone numbers, and the names of their family members and primary caregivers.
3. Make an ID card for each child and practice using it with others.

4. Send a letter home to parents so they know what you are working on at school. Emphasize that you are trying to teach all children to be safe.
5. Talk about the kinds of community helpers who assist children who are lost, such as police officers, medical personnel, and firefighters.

Reflect:

1. Reflect on which children you feel may be especially gullible and provide extra practice and reinforcement using the poster you created.
2. Think about ways you can help children learn to protect themselves.

TERMS USED IN THIS CHAPTER

curriculum—refers to both the content and composition of the classroom instruction. In other words, what is happening throughout a typical day?

curriculum model—a specific type of educational system that combines theory with practice and is usually based on some underlying philosophy, such as whole-child development or constructivist learning.

differentiated instruction—an approach to planning a lesson or activity, whereby, while a lesson is taught to the entire class, the individual needs of each child are also met.

recognition and response—similar to response to intervention (RTI) in that this strategy attempts to identify and respond to learning issues when they occur rather than waiting until the child is so far behind in his learning that special education is necessary. This is a proactive response.

response to intervention (RTI)—an emerging practice for diagnosing learning disabilities and learning needs in which a student with academic delays is given one or more research-validated interventions before they are significantly behind in their development. It is an alternative to the discrepancy model, which deals with learning differences after they are apparent for a long time.

RESOURCES USED IN THIS CHAPTER

Bernhard, J. K., Winsler, A., Bleiker, C., Ginieniewicz, J., & Madigan, A. (2005, April).*The early authors program: Implementing transformative literacy in early childhood education.* Paper presented at the annual meeting of the American Educational Research Association, Montreal, Quebec, Canada.

Dickinson, D. K., & Tabors, P. O. (2001). *Beginning literacy with language.* Baltimore, MD: Paul H. Brookes.

Fisch, R. O., Smith, M., & Phinney, M. Y. (1997). Project read: The importance of early learning. *American Family Physician, 56*(9), 2195–2198.

Hall, T., Strangman, N., & Meyer, A. (2003). *Differentiated instruction and implications for UDL implementation.* Wakefield, MA: National Center on Accessing the General Curriculum. Retrieved December 1, 2007, from http://www.cast.org/publications/ncac/ncac_diffinstructudl.html

Isbell, C., & Isbell, R. (2005). *The complete learning center book for preschool children with special needs.* Beltsville, MD: Gryphon House.

Juel, C. (2006). The impact of early school experiences on initial reading. In D. Dickinson, & S. B. Neuman (Eds.), *Handbook of Early Literacy Research* (Vol. 2). New York: The Guilford Press.

Mooney, C. G. (2005). *Use your words: How teacher talk helps students learn.* St. Paul, MN: Redleaf Press.

Snow, C. E., Burns, M. S., & Griffin, P. (Eds.). (1998). *Preventing reading difficulties in young children.* Washington, DC: National Academies Press.

SUGGESTED READING

MacDonald, S. (2007). *Math in minutes.* Beltsville, MD: Gryphon House.

McGee, L. M., & Richgels, D. J. (2003). *Designing early literacy programs.* New York: The Guilford Press.

McKenzie, M. A., Marchand-Martella, N. E., Moore, M. E., & Martella, R. C. (2004). Teaching basic math skills to preschoolers using "connecting math concepts level K." *Journal of Direct Instruction, 4*(1), 85–94.

Williams, R. A., Rockwell, R. F., & Sherwood, E. A. (1987). *Mudpies to magnets: A preschool science curriculum.* Beltsville, MD: Gryphon House.

Handling Challenging Behaviors

15

Figure 15.1   It is important for children to understand the natural consequence of their behavior.

WHAT IS CHALLENGING BEHAVIOR?

Children with special needs are just like other children in that all of the behaviors they exhibit occur for two reasons: (a) either to gain access to something they perceive as needed (toy, attention from adult, food, etc.) or (b) to avoid something that is undesirable (sitting in a circle for small group, waiting for a turn, complying with a rule, etc.). Children with challenging behaviors often demand the attention of adults thus creating a learning environment in which more time is spent dealing with these behaviors than developing much-needed social and content-related skills. In addition, teachers find themselves spending more time telling children what not to do rather than spending time helping children learn new skills (MacDonald, 2000). The following activities can help minimize the amount of time spent on dealing with challenging behaviors:

- Modeling appropriate behavior
- Offering choices
- Being proactive and making expectations clear, before challenging behaviors occur
- Verbally acknowledging positive behaviors
- Encouraging children to interact with others appropriately

WHAT KINDS OF BEHAVIORS CAN I TOLERATE?

It is important to note which behaviors can be tolerated (ignored) and which behaviors warrant your time and attention. Certainly, if a child is engaging in a behavior that could result in injury to himself or others (hitting another child, biting himself, etc.), it must be stopped immediately. On the other hand, if a child is engaging in a behavior that can be ignored (screaming out for the teacher, demanding to have a turn, etc.), ignoring it is often the best option. By ignoring certain behaviors, you are communicating to all of the children that you will not respond to unacceptable behaviors. Typically, the normal response to a challenging behavior is an action followed by a reaction. For example, Tyra wants to work a puzzle on the computer and Myron is currently working on the computer. Instead of asking Myron to quit, Tyra rushes forward and knocks Myron out of his chair. Myron starts to cry and the teacher reacts by sending Tyra to "time out." This "action leads to reaction" sequence results in Tyra being upset and angry, and Myron being unnecessarily knocked out of his chair. The scenario above could have been avoided if the teacher had been more proactive by redirecting Tyra to another activity before she approached Myron. Once a teacher determines the function behind a behavior, it will be easier to teach the child how to select an alternative way to respond that is less challenging or threatening to others. Had Tyra known a strategy to use (other than pushing Myron out of his chair), the scene could probably have been avoided. However, before the teacher can begin to teach Tyra, or any other child, a strategy for managing behavior, it will be necessary for the teacher to conduct a functional assessment.

WHAT IS A FUNCTIONAL ASSESSMENT?

A functional assessment is the process of determining the relationship between events in a person's environment and the occurrence of challenging behaviors (McEvoy, Reichle, & Davis, 1995). Simply stated, a functional assessment is an organized method by which the teacher or other professional determines why the behavior occurred. The process involves the following steps:

1. Identifying and defining the challenging behavior. This is accomplished by asking yourself what, specifically, the child does that can be defined as a challenging behavior.
2. Identifying the events and circumstances regularly associated with the occurrence and the nonoccurrence of the challenging behavior. This will help answer the question concerning the circumstances under which the behavior occurs and, more important, under what circumstances the behavior does not occur.
3. Determining the social function or purpose that brought about the challenging behavior (Foster-Johnson & Dunlap, 1993; O'Neill, Horner, Albin, Storey, & Sprague, 1990). The social function may be related to the child wanting more or less attention from another child or an adult.

Another important component in a functional analysis is the setting event that contributed to the behavior. Setting events are conditions that occur at the same time as problem behaviors or events that occurred recently enough to influence the behavior. A setting event is an event that is not routine and that increases the probability that a challenging behavior will occur. Setting events may include the following:

- Staff changes—Was the teacher absent yesterday? Does the child have a new caregiver after school?
- Medication change—Was the child's medication increased or decreased? Did the child's family forget to give her medication that day?
- Sleep habits—Is the child getting enough sleep at night? Does he sleep through the night?
- Illness—Remember, some children lack the language skills to tell you that they do not feel well, so they may throw something or hit another child out of frustration rather than anger.
- Stress—Has the child been placed in an environment that is more demanding for her?

- Chaotic environment—Has there been an unscheduled change in the daily schedule?
- Surprise visits—Did the child go to the doctor after school yesterday? Does the family suddenly have out-of-town company?
- Aggression by a peer—Has another child been teasing the child? Did another child physically hurt the child?
- Temperature changes—Children with sensory integration issues are very sensitive to changes in the environment; a classroom that is too cold or too warm can be very upsetting to them.
- Dissatisfaction with a specific event—Did the child have to wait too long to get something he wanted? Is something he enjoys (like the computer) broken so he cannot use it today?

Once the reason or function of a behavior has been established, another step must be taken before deciding on strategies to use, which help the child learn how to manage her own behavior. This step involves identifying what positive behaviors the child needs to develop to be successful at school and in her relationships with others.

IDENTIFICATION OF POSITIVE BEHAVIORS

In order to be successful in their relationships with others, all children should learn several important positive behaviors. These include the following:

- Trust—a sense of trust is developed when the child learns that his environment and the people in it are safe for him physically and emotionally.
- Social relationships—making, keeping, and being a friend to others.
- Managing feelings—knowing when he is feeling sad and why, or understanding why someone else feels differently than he does about something.

Figure 15.2   Reinforce positive behavior with a preferred activity.

- Motivation—having the initiative to try new things, feeling successful about new endeavors, and learning new skills. Nothing kills motivation more quickly than constant failure.
- Finding solutions to challenges—children who learn to solve and take responsibility for their own problems are less frustrated when new problems arise.
- Respect for others and themselves—it is important that children learn to respect others and themselves, as this leads to an emotionally healthy adulthood.

With these positive behavior skills in mind, let's look at some strategies that help children with special needs manage their own behavior while they work to develop essential positive behaviors.

Strategy

Communicative Replacement

Purpose: The purpose of this strategy is to offer the child a replacement for the current behavior by offering choices that are more acceptable than the current behavior.

Focus: When the child is behaving in a way that cannot be ignored, the first step is to stop the behavior before it happens again. For example, if Karen is screaming and throwing blocks at her peers, the teacher should approach Karen and say, "We don't throw blocks." The teacher should wait and see if Karen listens to what she says. If Karen continues to throw the blocks, then the teacher uses a physical assist (physically removing the blocks from Karen's reach) and directs Karen to look at her (the teacher). In the case of an extremely resistant child, the teacher may need to take the child's hands in her own for a few seconds.

Develop: Once the teacher has Karen's attention, the teacher's next step is to offer a choice. It is best to begin by offering two choices and eventually work up to offering three choices. The teacher may say, "Karen, you seem upset. Would you like to go with me and throw a ball, or would you like to sit down and play with these five blocks?" (handing her five smaller blocks). By giving the child a choice, the teacher is giving the child more control over her environment. The teacher is honoring the reason or function behind Karen's throwing of the blocks by giving her choice. The teacher is not honoring or condoning the behavior (throwing blocks) itself.

Practice: Look for opportunities throughout the school day to help the child practice making choices. Some children have not had much experience in making their own choices and therefore need extra help.

Reflect: It is also important for the teacher to reflect and identify situations in which choices cannot be offered. For example, if Marylee screams every day when it is time to eat lunch, the teacher has no alternative but to see that Marylee eats her lunch. Lunch is an essential daily routine and is not an optional activity. The teacher cannot offer the child the choice of not eating lunch. It will be necessary for the teacher to identify situations related to eating lunch that may enable making a choice. For example, the child could choose who she wants to sit with at lunch, or the child could choose where at the table she would like to sit. In some cases, the child may be able to select the color of the chair she sits in or the color or type of placemat that she eats her lunch on.

Strategy

Learning to Wait

Purpose: The purpose of this strategy is to encourage the child to stop a challenging behavior (screaming, hitting, etc.) that is caused by having to wait for something he wants.

Focus: Teaching the child to wait for something he wants is accomplished through two steps: (a) giving the child a cue that, if he waits, he will get what he wants or an acceptable alternative and (b) redirecting the child until such time as his desired activity is available to him.

Develop: Develop a cue that is specific to the child; use something that indicates you want him to stop his current behavior and wait. The cue may be as simple as counting to five or pointing to a stop sign. Redirect the child to something else that he enjoys, like a game, toy, or activity. Praise the child for stopping the challenging behavior. When his "waiting time" is over, continue to praise the child by congratulating him for waiting.

Practice: Look for opportunities throughout the day for the child to practice his waiting strategy. When you notice a peer who is waiting patiently, without interrupting the class, praise the peer as well. In addition, it is helpful to review and model the use of this strategy with the entire class from time to time. Waiting is a difficult task for a child without special needs and can be even more challenging for a child with special needs.

Reflect: Reflect on times when the child used this strategy effectively and make note of them in your anecdotal records. Ask yourself if there are times when it seems to be easier for the child to wait.

Strategy

I Think I Can! I Know I Can!—"The Little Engine that Could!"

Purpose: To encourage a child with special needs to keep trying an activity, even if that activity is difficult for her.

Focus: Children with special needs often give up and quit trying when they perceive that an activity is too difficult or challenging for them. This strategy stresses the importance of trying new activities. Focus the child's attention by telling her that you will be talking about trains. Show her a picture of a train or give her a toy train to explore.

Develop: Invite the child to sit with you while you read the story, *The Little Engine that Could!* (You will find several variations on the market.) Talk about why the engine kept trying, even though his task was very challenging. Invite the child to repeat key phrases after you, such as, "I think I can! I think I can!" This activity also lends itself well to small group instruction.

Practice: To help children reinforce the meaning behind the story, remind them throughout the day about how the little engine just kept trying. Look for ways to incorporate the story into your learning centers. For example, count the cars on the train in the math learning center, use sequence cards to help the children retell the story to each other in the literacy center, and draw trains in the art center. If possible, get some boxes and invite children to decorate them like trains. In the drama center, encourage children to reenact the story using the "pretend train" boxes.

Reflect: Look for ways to put up visual reminders for the child to "keep trying." Think about specific words or gestures you could use to let the child know that you are proud of her attempts.

Strategy

Rejecting an Optional Activity

Purpose: The purpose of this activity is to teach the child how to reject an activity or how to voice his displeasure with something in a socially acceptable manner.

Focus: Many challenging behaviors are the result of the child trying to express his displeasure with something or someone. For example, the child is trying to communicate, "NO!" emphatically, and does not know how to do so in a manner that expresses his feelings appropriately. When a child exhibits a challenging behavior, it is appropriate for the teacher to comment on "why" the child may be responding the way he is responding. For example, if the teacher indicates that it is time to stop playing and join the class in a large group activity, the child may respond to that by throwing a tantrum.

Develop: To help the child learn alternatives to challenging behaviors, the teacher may need to develop ways to help the child learn to show his displeasure either verbally or by using a cue or picture card. Talk about ways to say "no" that are acceptable, such as shaking the head or learning to use the sign for "no."

Practice: Help the child practice his alternative way to say "no." It may be necessary to remind him how to say "no" (word, gesture, sign, etc.) prior to his getting upset.

Reflect: Think about times when the child does say or sign "no" appropriately and try to identify the setting events that may have influenced him.

Strategy

Anger Management

Purpose: The purpose of this strategy is to help the child learn to manage her own anger by providing an alternative to physical violence.

Focus: Set up a "feelings center" in your classroom. In some cases, it might even be appropriate to call it an "anger center." Give the class a tour of the center (this is probably best accomplished by taking a few children at a time into the center) and explain that it is a place to go when a child gets mad or angry. Explain that everyone gets angry, but that hitting someone or throwing something at someone in anger is never an acceptable way to solve the problem. Demonstrate activities in the center: a place to pound clay, a place to wad up paper, special paper for scribbling, and so on.

Develop: Help children learn when to go to the anger or feelings center. During small group instruction, talk about things that make children mad. Talk about alternatives to being angry like counting out loud to 10 or wadding up paper and throwing it away. Talk about ways children can teach themselves to relax when they are angry, like taking deep breaths or thinking about "happy memories."

Practice: Provide practice using the anger or feelings center by redirecting a child to the center when you think the child is getting angry. Model for her the various activities that are there to help her manage, or get rid of, her anger.

Reflect: Reflect on how often the center is being used. Ask yourself if there are times when children are not using the anger or feelings center when they should be using it. Are there things you can do to help children have more access to the center?

TERMS USED IN THIS CHAPTER

challenging behaviors—problem behavior that interferes with the child's learning new skills.

functional assessment—the process of determining the relationship between events in a person's environment and the occurrence of challenging behaviors.

physical assist—removing an object of interest from the child when the child is displaying a challenging behavior.

setting events—conditions that happen concurrent with problem behaviors or events that happened recently enough that they could influence the behavior.

RESOURCES USED IN THIS CHAPTER

Foster-Johnson, L., Dunlap, G. (1993). Using functional assessment to develop effective individualized interventions for challenging behaviors. *Teaching Exceptional Children, 25*(4), 44–50.

MacDonald, L. (2000). *Learning interrupted: Maladaptive behavior in the classroom.* Retrieved December 13, 2005, from http://www.mugsy .org

McEvoy, M., Reichle, J., & Davis, C. (1995). *Challenging behaviors in young children.* Minneapolis, MN: Minnesota Behavioral Support Project.

O'Neill, R.E., Horner, R.H., Albin, R., Storey, K., & Sprague, J. (1990). *Functional assessment of problem behavior: A practical assessment guide.* Pacific Grove, CA: Brookes.

SUGGESTED READING

Bilmes, J. (2004). *Beyond behavior management: The six life skills children need to thrive in today's world.* St. Paul, MN: Redleaf Press.

Fouse, B., & Wheeler, M. (1997). *A treasure chest of behavior strategies.* Arlington, TX: Future Horizons.

Reichle, J. (1991). Challenging behavior. *Impact, 4*(1), 1–19.

Van der Kolk, B., Perry, J., & Herman, J. (1991). Childhood origins of self-destructive behavior. *American Journal of Psychiatry, 148,* 1665–1671.

Building Communication   16

Figure 16.1   Nonverbal children use pictures to interact.

UNDERSTANDING COMMUNICATION

As previously mentioned, *communication* is about sending and receiving messages. To plan effectively for the communication needs of children with special needs, it is important to know at which stage of communication development the child currently functions. The important thing to remember is that before a child can effectively communicate, he must have the tools he needs to do so and he must know how to use those tools. Communication goes far beyond just knowing how to talk; it involves the child having a reason or motivation to communicate as well. The first step in planning for communication is to recognize the various levels of communication and determine which level best describes the child's current level of functioning (Sussman, 1999).

LEVELS OF COMMUNICATION DEVELOPMENT

The various levels of communication have been given a variety of names and defined in many ways. While each child is unique in her communication development, most children, even children with special needs, will move sequentially through these levels, including the following:

1. "It's all about me" (egocentric)—At this level, the child's primary goal is to get her needs met.
2. "I want it" (requesting)—This is the level when the child begins to request and ask for things using language as a means to tell others what he wants.
3. "Actions and reactions" (emerging communication)—A child at this level is emerging in her communication and begins experimenting with language and words more creatively.
4. "Two-way street" (reciprocal communication)—In this stage, the child has learned that communication is about both sending and receiving information. It goes without saying that this is the level at which most teachers would like to see young children communicate.

The first, egocentric ("It's all about me"), level usually occurs around age 2. Children with special needs may communicate at this level in preschool or kindergarten. During this stage of communication, the child's main intent is very self-directed. He uses whatever method is available to him (pointing, gesturing, speaking, or even screaming) to let you know what he wants and needs. Children in this stage may communicate by

- reaching out to an adult with his hands to indicate "I want";
- screaming or throwing a tantrum when the adults around him don't give her what he wants;
- smiling when someone looks at him;
- being open with those he knows and being very shy around strangers and new people;
- interacting with adults who are familiar to him, rather than his peers; and
- repeating phrases over and over just for fun.

The second, requesting ("I want it"), level occurs as the child learns about cause and effect. She begins to understand that what she says or does has an effect on people or on her environment. During this stage, a child starts to see communication as a means to get what she wants. She begins to learn that communication is a tool she can use to request things from others. If the adults in her world cooperate by giving her what she requests, then she learns that language is a much better method to use than screaming or crying. Children in this stage may communicate by

- grabbing your hand and pulling you toward something she wants;
- saying a few basic words, in an effort to let you know what she wants;
- moving her body, when you are interacting with her, to communicate "I want more";
- learning to sign the word "more" by putting her hands together; and
- approximating words or attempting a few new words.

Children who function at the third, emerging communication ("Actions and reactions"), level are beginning to use communication in a more functional way. They are starting to understand that repeating the same words or actions get the same results. Children in this stage will put two words together and seem to enjoy repeating what they just heard. The communication interactions that occur with the child are much longer and more sustained than at the previous levels. Emerging communicators will communicate by

- taking turns with others;
- understanding the names of those familiar to him;
- repeating what he just heard;
- using gestures more consistently such as shaking his head "no";
- answering simple questions—especially yes/no questions;
- asking for something or requesting the continuation of an activity; and
- using words or signs in more meaningful ways.

The fourth, reciprocal communication ("two-way street"), level is characterized by more direct communication with a partner. In this stage, children begin to recognize that communication is reciprocal in nature. Children in this stage are often more prone to communicate with adults than with peers. While children with more significant needs may continue to have difficulty with initiating or beginning conversations with peers, children at this stage may participate in a conversation if they have a strong need or a motivation to get something from the other child. Spontaneous initiation in many children with special needs does not happen naturally. Children in this level of communication may have difficulty with social cues, new social situations, and understanding the abstracts of language such as with jokes. Children in this reciprocal communication stage communicate by

- intentionally using words to greet, ask for something, or protest something;
- asking questions and describing important events;
- expressing ideas and feelings that are relevant to them;
- having short conversations;
- repeating something if they think the listener does not understand; and
- starting to use longer sentences with more descriptive words.

HOW DO YOU SET APPROPRIATE GOALS FOR COMMUNICATION?

It is often difficult to know how to plan activities when a child is learning to communicate. It is equally challenging to know what to expect from a child with developmental delays. While each child is unique and communicates in her own way, several general guidelines can be considered when planning activities:

1. Learning to interact with other people is a life skill that the child can build on and use throughout her life. Therefore, learning to communicate with others should always be a top priority for every child.
2. To communicate effectively, the child must have a reliable way to communicate. This means that if the child is nonverbal, alternative methods must be considered.
3. The ultimate goal for any child is to learn to communicate because it is meaningful to her. You want the child with special needs to communicate more than telling others what she wants and needs. You want her to learn to use communication as a form of self-expression.
4. Communication should be meaningful. Help the child with special needs use communication as a way to connect her world with that of her peers.

In addition to the general guidelines just mentioned, Table 16.1 lists some communication goals based on the child's stage of communication:

Table 16.1   Communication Goals Based on the Child's Stage of Communication

Stage of Communication	Goals
Level 1 Egocentric ("It's all about me")	1. Insist that the child show you what he wants by pointing, gesturing, or using sign language. 2. Play simple games that involve taking turns. Verbalize what you are doing. Say, "It is my turn," and point to yourself. Then say, "It is your turn," and point to the child. 3. Verbalize what the child is doing. 4. Respond to every communication attempt even if it is unintentional; this reinforces the child's efforts to communicate.
Level 2 Requesting ("I want it")	1. Play a game, or start an activity. Then, stop and try to get the child to request "more," by the child either moving her body or looking at you. 2. When the child pulls you toward something or points to a desired object, say the name of the object, then smile. 3. Use simple sentences to describe everything the child does. 4. Children with language delays often respond poorly to continuous talk. They are underresponsive to verbal stimuli. Provide a model by saying it from a child's point of view. Wait expectantly and give the child time to respond.
Level 3 Emerging Communication ("Actions and reactions")	1. Continue to play games that involve "taking-turns," while encouraging the child to play with other children. 2. Provide an exact model of what you want the child to say and do. 3. Respond to any situations where the child initiates a communication interaction. 4. Build the child's vocabulary, by giving him experiences that will help him develop new words. 5. If the child is using pictures to communicate, also encourage him to use words if possible.
Level 4 Reciprocal Communication ("Two-way street")	1. Set up classroom situations that encourage conversations between children. 2. The environment plays a major role in helping children interact. So set up a classroom that encourages communication. 3. Play games where you practice the rules of conversation, such as starting, stopping, and waiting a turn. 4. Help the child use communication for more than just simple requests; talk about communicating feelings or opinions. 5. Ask other children in the classroom to be peer buddies and talk with the child.

WHAT ABOUT CHILDREN WHO ARE NONVERBAL?

Some children with special needs will never use spoken language as their primary form of communication. For these children, it may be necessary to use an alternative or augmentative form of communication. These augmentative forms of communication generally fall into two categories: low-tech and high-tech. Low-tech methods of communication include pictures or objects that the child either points to or selects as a way to tell you what he wants or needs. High-tech communication methods generally involve a battery-operated device that the child activates in some manner or a computer that talks for the child.

LOW-TECH METHODS OF COMMUNICATION

While sign language is certainly one method that can be functional for a nonverbal child, pictures are clearly more universal. Anyone, including a child's peer, can understand that if a child with special needs points to a picture of a toy, it means she would like to play with the toy. Handing a picture to a communication partner is one way the child can interact with that partner. Pictures are used in various ways:

- To make communication boards
- For schedules including embedded schedules
- In combinations in an effort to describe concepts and ideas
- To indicate a choice or a preference
- As an answer to a question

Pictures are not only practical and simple to use, but they also provide a sense of consistency since the same set of pictures used at school can also be used at home. When using a picture communication system, you will want to refer to the guidelines in Table 16.2.

Table 16.2   Guidelines for Using a Picture Communication System

General uses for pictures	• To help the child learn daily routines • To sequence an activity • To introduce a new word • To provide an added clue for children with special needs
Pictures as a way to initiate a conversation with someone	• Once the child becomes more familiar with the pictures in the classroom, try to encourage him to use them to start a communication interaction • Model using pictures with small groups of children

Consistently use the same pictures with each individual child	• Consistency and practice will reinforce the child's use of the picture cards • Send pictures home and encourage the child's family to use them too
Continually build opportunities for the child to use and expand her vocabulary and skills through pictures	• Ask questions that require the child to answer you by pointing to a picture • Expand the child's repertoire of pictures, by including action pictures and pictures that can be used to tell you what and how the child is feeling

HOW DO I START HELPING A CHILD WITH SPECIAL NEEDS USE PICTURES TO COMMUNICATE?

The most widely recognized formal system of communication is the Picture Exchange System (PECS) developed by Andy Bondy and Lori Frost. PECS can be purchased from Pyramid Education Products, Inc. at http://www.pyramidproducts.com. In the PECS system, a child presents pictures to a partner or selects pictures from a board or portable notebook. The pictures are inexpensive and portable, allowing the child to use them in a variety of different situations. While pictures are an excellent teaching tool for children with special needs, using the official PECS system requires special training because there is a specific method to presenting each sequence of pictures.

An alternative might be a simple communication board that uses laminated pictures taken with a digital camera. A *communication board* is a tool that can easily be used by a child who does not have verbal communication skills (Gould & Sullivan, 1999). Start out using one or two pictures and work up to using more. Experiment to determine whether the child responds best to real pictures or to black-and-white line drawings. This is important because some children with special needs have difficulty understanding that a drawing is a representation of a real object. In some cases, a child might not respond to either pictures or drawings and it will be necessary to use real objects instead of pictures.

WHAT ABOUT ELECTRONIC COMMUNICATION DEVICES?

why?

Traditionally, young children with special needs do not use high-end electronic communication devices. However, a few products can be used appropriately with young children. These include devices with the capacity to deliver one message or, in some cases, devices that can be programmed to deliver several messages.

PICTURE SCHEDULES

What is a picture schedule?

- Vertical or horizontal strip of pictures that provides a display of what will happen
- Usually sequential and goes from the first event to the last event
- Contains pockets or uses Velcro so pictures can be changed frequently

Why use a picture schedule?

- To improve receptive language skills (the understanding of language)
- To let the child know what will happen next, thus reducing challenging behaviors
- To use as a supplement with verbal directions to reinforce following a command
- To increase understanding of new vocabulary
- To aid in learning how to do a particular task
- To help teach the concept of sequencing and ordinal terms (first, next, last...)
- To promote independence, by reinforcing a child with special needs to complete tasks without adult assistance

What is an embedded schedule?

- The specific activities are presented sequentially, going horizontally across the board, to make the schedule. Then, the steps for a particular activity are presented vertically.
- For example, if the third picture is "bathroom time," then vertically, below the picture of the bathroom, are pictures depicting the steps the child needs to perform while in the bathroom.

Hints

- Start out using only a few pictures.
- Remind the child that the schedule tells her what will happen next.
- Until the child becomes more familiar with the picture schedule, the teacher will need to prompt her in how to use it.

Single message switches, such as the "Big-Mack Jellybean Switch" by Ablenet, are sometimes used to help children, as they begin to communicate. It is a button-type switch on which a single message has been recorded. The child is taught to push the button and the message is spoken. Unlike the more expensive devices, this switch can be used with multiple children and often is a great tool when children are learning to let you know they need to go to the bathroom. A picture of a bathroom or a toilet can easily be taped or attached to the switch. Whenever any child needs to go, they just walk up to the switch and push the button. The message is easily changed and the device is easy to operate.

Multiple message devices include the "Speak-Easy" or the "Talking Communication Book." These electronic devices enable more than one message to be recorded. In addition, they are easy to use, and the messages can be changed when necessary. Regardless of which device is used, it is very important that the teacher start by teaching the child to use only one or two messages and gradually add more as the child learns to use the device more independently. If a child comes into your classroom with an electronic device, a few guidelines should be considered:

1. Be sure the recorded voice on the device is a child's voice and not the voice of an adult.
2. Contact the manufacturer of the device. Most of the manufacturers are happy to provide a free demonstration for teachers, or at the very least, provide you with material about how the device works.
3. Find out what size batteries the device uses and keep plenty on hand.
4. Remember that the device belongs to the child. It is his voice and is not a toy to be used by other children.

Strategy

A Communication Apron

Purpose: The purpose of this strategy is to help teachers facilitate use of pictures as a form of communication.

Focus: Make a communication apron by using Velcro® to attach key pictures to an apron. You can purchase a chef's apron or you can make one.

Develop:

1. Begin by selecting one or two keywords. Remember to select functional words that the child will use consistently at school, home, or in the community.

2. Find or take a photograph that represents each word.

3. Use the apron as a tool to help you facilitate the child's use of pictures.

4. Once a child becomes familiar with a word on the apron, others may be added.

Figure 16.2 Teachers can use a communication apron to display pictures.
Illustration by Justin Mitchel

Practice:

1. Give children with special needs the opportunity to practice pointing to or using each word on your apron.
2. Plan activities that involve the child using these pictures for communication.
3. For nonverbal children with special needs, make it a priority that they learn to use pictures whenever they communicate.
4. Use pictures with children who are verbal as well. Remember, the use of pictures will only enhance the child's communication. If a child has the capacity to use words verbally, but has not yet mastered the skill of using words effectively, this will help bridge the gap until he does.

Reflect:

1. Children with special needs will need extra practice, so think about ways you can incorporate using the same pictures within daily routines.

2. Children with special needs can develop learned helplessness if everything is done for them. Insist that a child lets you know what he wants or needs.

Strategy

Asking for a Work Break (Learning to Make Appropriate Requests)

Purpose: A request for a break is a strategy in which the child completes a portion of an activity and then requests a break. Following the break, the child returns to the activity and completes it. It is very important that the child return and attempt to finish the original activity, or the child learns to manipulate the environment by requesting a work break as a method of "getting out" of doing specific activities that she does not enjoy.

Focus: A request for a break is a communicative intervention in which the child completes a portion of an activity and then requests a break. This request may be in the form of a spoken word, a gesture, or sign language. Following the break, the child returns to the activity.

Develop: These steps help the child learn to use this task effectively:

1. Request the work break—a request for a break may be accomplished by using spoken language (asking), a gesture (raising a hand, palm outward, to indicate "stop"), or pointing to a picture (a stop sign).
2. Acknowledge the request—once the child has indicated that she wants a break, the teacher acknowledges her request with a gesture (nod yes) or a verbal answer.
3. Determining the time allowed for the break—the teacher then sets a timer, which determines the amount of time that will be allowed for the break. Hour-glass timers usually are more effective than timers that ring because, for many children, the ringing is very distracting.
4. Determining the location for the break—the child then goes to a pre-specified location (quiet center, comfortable chair, etc.) for the duration of the break.

5. When the break is over—after a break, the teacher directs the child to return to "work." If the child is noncompliant, the teacher escorts the child back to the area designated for her to complete the original activity.

Practice: It is important to model this strategy for the child so that she understands each step. One way to model this is to ask a peer to act out each step as you describe it. Another method to help the child know what to do is to provide picture sequence cards that show what to do first, second, and so on. Remember, children with special needs may require additional practice using this strategy before they understand when and how to use it.

Reflect: Look for ways to help the child see the benefits associated with this strategy. Place the sequence cards in the literacy area of your classroom and encourage the child to put them in correct sequence. Invite the child to demonstrate each step of the process. If this strategy is not working, look for ways to motivate the child to try it. You or your assistant may have to take a "break" along with the child, the first couple of times, until she understands how the strategy works.

Strategy

Working Together—Collaboration Is Fun!

Purpose: The purpose of this activity is to increase the likelihood that a child will complete an activity, while offering an opportunity for children to learn together and communicate with one another.

Focus: Collaboration is a strategy in which the responsibilities of an activity are divided between a child and another individual (peer or adult). Collaboration is effective in reducing challenging behavior and increasing engagement in tasks, because it decreases the task demands placed on the child.

Develop: Develop this strategy by selecting an activity that the child with special needs will find particularly enjoyable. Remember to limit the work groups to two or three children, so that no one feels overwhelmed or left out of the activity. Initially, the child with special needs may not want to participate and it may be necessary for you to help him or allow him to observe until he is more comfortable.

Practice: The more a child gets to practice working with others, the less he will be resistant to the idea. While you cannot guarantee that all collaboration will be fun and rewarding, it is very important that the initial collaborations are positive experiences for all involved. Remember to send notes home telling families about your classroom collaborations and encouraging them to praise the child for his participation. Before inviting the child to participate in collaboration, model each step of the activity for him and review any vocabulary related to the activity which may be unfamiliar to him. It will be much easier for the child to participate when he knows what is expected of him.

Reflect: Observe the children in your class and note who the most effective collaborators might be. Identify who is more tolerant of others and who is more patient with peers. Praise children when you see that they are collaborating well with each other. Use phrases like, "Josh and Tanya, you guys are painting such a beautiful picture together" or "Micah and Tameka, you make a great team!"

TERMS USED IN THIS CHAPTER

approximating—when a word is pronounced in a way that is close to but not exactly correct

communication—the reciprocal process of sending and receiving information

communication board—a board or poster which uses either pictures or drawings to represent objects or concepts that the child might need to communicate about

RESOURCES USED IN THIS CHAPTER

Gould, P., & Sullivan, J. (1999). *The inclusive early childhood classroom: Easy ways to adapt learning centers for all children.* Beltsville, MD: Gryphon House.

Sussman, F. (1999). *More than words.* Toronto, Ontario, Canada: Hanen Center.

SUGGESTED READING

Chen, D., Klein D. M., & Haney. (2000). *Promoting learning through active interaction: A guide to early communication with young children who have multiple disabilities.* Baltimore: Paul H. Brookes.

Johnston, S. S., McDonnell, A. P., Nelson, C., & Magnavito, A. (2003). Teaching functional communication skills using augmentative and alternative communication in inclusive settings. *Journal of Early Intervention, 25*(4).

Parette, P., & McMahan, G. A. (2002). What should we expect of assistive technology: Being sensitive to family goals. *Teaching Exceptional Children, 23*(1), 56–61.

Rowland, C. (1996). *Communication matrix: A communication skill assessment for individuals at the earliest stages of communication development.* Portland: Oregon Health Sciences University.

Appendix

Children's Books That Feature Dynamic Characters With Special Needs

Adapted from the National Dissemination Center for Children with Disabilities (NICHCY), PO Box 1492, Washington, DC 20013. Additional books added by the author.

Autism

Amenta, C. A., III. (1992). *Russell is extra special: A book about autism for children*. Washington, DC: Magination Press. (Ages 4–8)

Branon, B. (1998). *Timesong*. Las Vegas, NV: Huntington Press.

Hoopmann, K. (2006). *All cats have Asperger's syndrome*. London: Jessica Kingsley.

Katz, I., Ritvo, E., & Borowitz, F. (Illust.). (1993). *Joey and Sam*. West Hills, CA: Real Life Storybooks. (Grades K–6)

Landalf, H., & Rimland, M. (Illust.). (1998). *Secret night world of cats*. Lyme, NH: Smith & Kraus. (Grades K–3; The illustrator of this book has autism.)

Simmons, K. L. (1996). *Little rainman*. Arlington, TX: Future Horizons. (Ages 4–8)

Sprecher, J., & Forrest, J. (Illust.). (1997). *Jeffrey and the despondent dragon.* Muskego, WI: Special Kids. (Grades K–4)

Thompson, M. (1996). *Andy and his yellow Frisbee.* Bethesda, MD: Woodbine House. (Grades K–5)

Down Syndrome

Carter, A. R., Young, D. (Illust.), & Carter, C. (Illust.). (1997). *Big brother Dustin.* Morton Grove, IL: Albert Whitman. (Ages 4–8)

Carter, A. R., Young, D. (Photographer), & Carter, C. (Illust.). (1999). *Dustin's big school day.* Morton Grove, IL: Albert Whitman. (Ages 4–8)

Fleming, V. (1993). *Be good to Eddie Lee.* New York: Putnam. (Grades preschool–3)

Rickert, J. E., & McGahan, P. (Photographer). (1999). *Apple tree surprise.* Bethesda, MD: Woodbine House. (Ages 3–7)

Rickert, J. E., & McGahan, P. (Photographer). (1999). *Russ and the firehouse.* Bethesda, MD: Woodbine House. (Ages 3–7)

Rickert, J. E., & McGahan, P. (Photographer). (2001). *Russ and the almost perfect day.* Bethesda, MD: Woodbine House. (Ages 3–7)

Stuve-Bodeen, S. (1998). *We'll paint the octopus red.* Bethesda, MD: Woodbine House. (Ages 3–7)

Hearing Impairment, Including Deafness

Addabbo, C. (1998). *Dina the deaf dinosaur.* Stamford, CT: Hannacroix Creek. (Grades preschool–5; The author of this book is deaf.)

Booth, B., & Lamarche, J. (1991). *Mandy.* New York: Lothrop. (Ages 5–9; Hearing impairment)

Hodges, C., & Yoder, D. (Illust.). (1995). *When I grow up.* Hollidaysburg, PA: Jason & Nordic. (Grades K–4; Deafness)

Lowell, G. R., & Brooks, K. S. (Illust.). (2000). *Elana's ears, or how I became the best big sister in the world.* Washington, DC: Magination Press. (Ages 3–8; Deafness)

Slier, D. (1995). *Word signs.* Washington, DC: Gallaudet University Press. (Deafness)

Physical Disabilities

Carter, A. R., & Carter, C. S. (Photographer.). (2000). *Stretching ourselves: Kids with cerebral palsy.* Morton Grove, IL: Albert Whitman. (Ages 5–9)

Heelan, J. R. (1998). *Making of my special hand: Madison's story.* Atlanta, GA: Peachtree. (Ages 4–8; This book is about the making of a prosthesis.)

Heelan, J. R. (2000). *Rolling along: The story of Taylor and his wheelchair.* Atlanta, GA: Peachtree. (Ages 6–10; This book is about a boy with cerebral palsy learning to use a wheelchair.)

Holcomb, N. (1992). *Andy finds a turtle.* Hollisdayburg, PA: Jason & Nordic. (Grades preschool–2)

Holcomb, N. (1992). *Andy opens wide.* Hollisdayburg, PA: Jason & Nordic. (Grades preschool–2)

Holcomb, N. (1992). *Fair and square.* Hollisdayburg, PA: Jason & Nordic. (Grades preschool–2)

Myers, C., & Morgan, C. (Illust.). (1999). *Rolling along with Goldilocks and the three bears.* Bethesda, MD: Woodbine House. (Ages 3–7; Using a wheelchair)

Useman, S., Useman, E., & Pillo, C. (Illust.). (1999). *Tibby tried it.* Washington, DC: Magination Press. (Ages 3–8; This book is about a bird who can't fly.)

Serious Medical or Life-Threatening Conditions

Hamilton, V. (1999). *Bluish.* New York: Blue Sky Press. (Grades 2–6; Leukemia and using a wheelchair)

Harshman, M. (1995). *The storm.* New York: Cobblehill/Dutton. (Grades 2–6; Using a wheelchair)

Katz, I. (1994). *Uncle Jimmy.* West Hills, CA: Real Life Storybooks. (Grades K–6; AIDS)

Kübler-Ross, E. (1995). *Remember the secret* (Rev. ed.). Berkeley, CA: Celestial Arts. (Grades 1–4; About dying)

Mills, J. C. (1993). *Gentle willow: A story for children about dying.* Washington, DC: Magination Press. (Grades preschool–3)

Mills, J., & Chesworth, M. (Illust.). (1992). *Little tree: A story for children with serious medical problems.* Washington, DC: Magination Press. (Ages 4–8; Amputation)

Verniero, J. C., & Flory, V. (Illust.). (1995). *You can call me Willy: A story for children about AIDS.* Washington, DC: Magination Press. (Ages 4–8)

Sibling Issues

Lowell, G. R., & Brooks, K. S. (Illust.). (2000). *Elana's ears, or how I became the best big sister in the world.* Washington, DC: Magination Press. (Ages 3–8; Deafness)

Meyer, D. J. (Ed.). (1997). *Views from our shoes: Growing up with a brother or sister with special needs.* Bethesda, MD: Woodbine House. (Grades 3 and up)

Prizant, B. M. (Ed.). (1997). *In our own words: Stories by brothers and sisters of children with autism and PDD.* Fall River, MA: Adsum. (Ages 12 and up)

Thompson, M. (1992). *My brother Matthew.* Bethesda, MD: Woodbine House. (Grades K–5; About disability in general)

Visual Impairment, Including Blindness

Chamberlin, K. (1997). *Night search.* Hollisdayburg, PA: Jason & Nordic. (Also available in Braille)

Day, S., & Morris, D. (Illust.). *Luna and the big blur.* Washington, DC: Magination Press. (Ages 4–8)

Martin, B., Jr., Archambault, J., & Rand, T. (Illust.). (1995). *Knots on a counting rope.* New York: Henry Holt. (Grades preschool–2)

Schulman, A. (1997). *T.J.'s story: A book about a boy who is blind.* Minneapolis, MN: Lerner. (Ages 8–12)

Turk, R. (1998). *Doll on the top shelf.* Los Altos, CA: Owl's House Press. (Grades K–3; Book is presented in text and Braille)

Other

Buehrens, A., & Buehrens, C. (1991). *Adam and the magic marble: A magical adventure.* Duarte, CA: Hope Press. (Grades K–10; Tourette syndrome and cerebral palsy)

Carlisle, K. (1994). *Special raccoon: Helping a child learn about handicaps and love*. Far Hills, NJ: New Horizon. (About disability in general)

Gosselin, K. (1996). *Zooallergy: A fun story about allergy and asthma triggers*. Valley Park, MO: JayJo Books. (Grades K–6; Asthma and allergy testing)

Gosselin, K. (1998). *ABCs of asthma: An asthma alphabet book for kids of all ages*. Valley Park, MO: JayJo Books. (Grades K–5; Asthma)

Gosselin, K. (1998). *Taking diabetes to school* (2nd ed.). Valley Park, MO: JayJo Books. (Grades K–5; Diabetes)

Koplow, L., & Velasquez, E. (Illust.). (1991). *Tanya and the Tobo man: A story for children entering therapy*. Washington, DC: Magination Press. (Ages 4–8; Written in both English and Spanish)

Maguire, A. (1995). *We're all special*. Santa Monica, CA: Portunus. (Grades preschool and up; About disability in general)

Mulder, L., & Friar, J. H. (Illust.). (1992). *Sarah and Puffle: A story for children about diabetes*. Washington, DC: Magination Press. (Ages 4–8; Diabetes)

Roy, J. R. (1999). *Bed potatoes: An activity guide for kids who feel yukky, miserable, and just plain sick*. Saratoga Springs, NY: Activate Press.

Snyder, H., & Beebe, S. (Illust.). (1998). *Elvin: The elephant who forgets*. Wake Forest, NC: L&A Publishing. (Grades K–5; Traumatic brain injury)

Resources for Special Needs Products

(This is not intended to be an exhaustive list. Rather, it is to serve as a guide where products specifically designed for children with special needs may be found.)

FlagHouse, Inc. (Special Needs Products and Toys)
PO Box 109
Hasbrouck Heights, NJ 07604-3116
Web: flaghouse.com

Innovative Products, Inc. (Special Needs Products)
830 S. 48th Street
Grand Forks, ND 58201
Phone: 800-950-5185 (toll-free)
E-mail: jsteinke@iphope.com
Web: iphope.com

Special Needs Toy Company (Special Needs Toys)
4537 Gibsonia Road
Gibsonia, PA 15044
Phone: 800-467-6222 (toll-free)
Web: www.specialneedstoys.com

Comfort House (Adaptive Eating Utensils)
Order Desk
189-V Frelinghuysen Avenue
Newark, NJ 07114-1595
Web: comforthouse.com

The Wright Stuff, Inc. (Adaptive Eating Utensils & General Life Skills
   Materials)
135 Floyd G. Harrell Drive
Grenada, MS 38901
Phone: 877-750-0376
E-mail: info@thewright-stuff.com
Web: thewright-stuff.com

Battat, Inc. (Finger Crayons and Adaptive Art Materials)
44 Martina Circle
Plattsburgh, NY 12901-0149
Phone: 518-562-2200
E-mail: sales@battat-toys.com
Web: battattoys.com

Blick Art Materials (Adaptive Crayons, Paintbrushes, and Scissors)
PO Box 1267
Galesburg, IL 61402-1267
Phone: 800-933-2542 (toll-free)
E-mail: info@dickblick.com
Web: www.dickblick.com

ACB Radio (Internet Radio for Persons Who Are Blind)
United States
E-mail: support@acbradio.org
Web: www.acbradio.org

EnableMart (Low Vision Aids)
4210 E 4th Plain Boulevard
Vancouver, WA 98661
Phone: 888-640-1999 (toll-free)
Web: www.enablemart.com

Enhanced Vision Headquarters (Low Vision Aids)
5882 Machine Drive
Huntington Beach, CA 92649
Phone: 714-374-1829
Web: enhancedvision.com

Independent Living Aids, Inc. (Devices for Independent Living)
200 Robbins Lane
Jericho, NY 11753
Phone: 800-537-2118 (toll-free)
Web: www.independentliving.com
Audio Books/Large-Print Books

National Association for Visually Handicapped (Audio Books)
22 West 21st Street
New York, NY 10010
Phone: 888-205-5951 (toll-free)
Phone: 212-889-3141
E-mail: staff@navh.org
Web: navh.org

**National Library Service for the Blind and Physically
    Handicapped** (Large-Print/Audio Books)
Library of Congress
1291 Taylor Street NW
Washington, DC 20011
Phone: 888-657-7323 (toll-free)
Phone: 800-424-8567 (toll-free)
TDD: 202-707-0744
E-mail: nls@loc.gov
Web: www.loc.gov/nls

National Braille Press
Web: www.nbp.org

Seedlings Braille Books
Web: seedlings.org

American Foundation for the Blind
Web: afb.org

American Printing House for the Blind
Web: aph.org

Customized Large-Print Books

Huge Print Press
North Central Plaza I
12655 N. Central Expressway, Suite 416
Dallas, TX 75243
Phone: 866-484-3774 (toll-free)
Phone: 972-701-8288
Fax: 972-701-8088
E-mail: info@hugeprint.com
Web: hugeprint.com

Motor Adaptations and Adaptive Devices (Switches, Communication, Battery Interrupter)

AbleNet, Inc.
2808 Fairview Avenue North
Roseville, MN 55113-1308
Phone: 800-322-0956 U.S. and Canada (toll-free)
Phone: 651-294-2200
Fax: 651-294-2259 (business)
Fax: 651-294-2222 (orders)
Web: ablenetinc.com

Don Johnston, Inc.
26799 West Commerce Drive
Volo, IL 60073
Phone: 800-999-4660 U.S. and Canada (toll-free)
E-mail: info@donjohnston.com
Web: www.donjohnston.com

Tash, Inc.
3512 Mayland Court
Richmond, VA 23233
Phone: 800-463-5685 (toll-free)
E-mail: tashinc@aol.com
Web: tash.org

Attainment Company, Inc.
504 Commerce Parkway
PO Box 930160
Verona, WI 53593-0160
Phone: 800-327-4269 (toll-free)
Web: attainmentcompany.com

Mayer-Johnson, LLC

PO Box 1579
Solana Beach, CA 92075-7579
Phone: 800-588-4548 (toll-free)
Phone: 858-550-0084
FAX: 858-550-0449
Web: www.mayer-johnson.com

Abilitations

PO Box 922668
Norcross, GA 30010-2668
Phone: 800-850-8602 (toll-free)
Web: www.abilitations.com

Ball Dynamics International, LLC

14215 Mcad Street
Longmont, CO 80504
Phone: 800-752-2255 (toll-free)
Fax: 877-223-2962 (toll-free)
E-mail: orders@balldynamics.com
Web: www.balldynamics.com

FlagHouse, Inc.

601 FlagHouse Drive
Hasbrouck Heights, NJ 07604-3116
Web: flaghouse.com

Hearing Impaired (Group Amplifiers and Other Devices for the Classroom)

Precision Acoustics

501 Fifth Ave, Suite 704
New York, NY 10017
Phone: 212-986-6470

Enabling Devices

385 Warburton Avenue
Hastings-On-Hudson, NY 10706
Phone: 800-832-8697 (toll-free)
Phone: 914-478-0960
FAX: 914-478-7030
E-mail: sales@enablingdevices.com
Web: enablingdevices.com

Phonic Ear, Inc.
3880 Cypress Drive
Petaluma, CA 94954-7600
Phone: 800-227-0735 (toll-free)
Phone: 707-769-1110
Fax: 707-769-9624
E-mail: customerservice@phonicear.com
Web: www.phonicear.com

Doll With Down Syndrome Features

Downi Creations, Inc.
410 Steeple Crest North
Irmo, SC 29063
Phone: 888-749-9330 (toll-free)
Phone: 803-749-9330
E-mail: downi96@aol.com
Web: downicreations.com

Index